Strategic Leadership

Discover Your Map - Empower Your Future

Other works from Dr. Thompson

STAR Performance
Uniting Planning and Doing for a High Performance Leadership Model
Discover the fundamental relationship between strategy, tactics, action, and results. Learn to unify each of these critically important aspects of performance to achieve STAR Performance.

Leadership
2Xalt
Performance

Leadership Letters
This periodic production of 2Xalt, Inc. features helpful tips and articles on leadership. Visit 2Xalt.com today to subscribe.

Martial Art of Performance
STAR Leadership Certification
Learn the principles of strategic leadership, tactical leadership, and performance leadership and how professional coaching can help integrate these principles in lasting ways. Earn your Green Belt, Brown Belt, and Black Belt in STAR Leadership. Visit 2Xalt.com to learn how.

Centurion Living
Life Planning Fundamentals
Discover the real meaning of life, and how to live with purpose and a mission. Develop an understanding of the difference between purpose and mission, and how to apply each to your daily living for powerful, life-changing results.

Strategic Leadership

Discover Your Map - Empower Your Future

Justin Thompson, PhD

2Xalt Press books may be ordered through booksellers or by contacting:

2Xalt Press
An Imprint of 2Xalt, Inc.
Viera, FL 32955
www.2Xalt.com
+1.321.430.4258

Excellent discounts on quantity orders for bulk purchases or special sales are available from 2Xalt Press. Order a box today for use in training programs, NPO fundraisers, corporate gifts, book sales, and other events. Visit 2Xalt.com/Press for more information, or call us at the number above.

2Xalt Press provides a range of authors and subject matter experts for speaking events. To learn more, visit 2Xalt.com/Press or call +1.321.430.4258.

Because of the dynamic nature of the Internet, any web addresses or links contained in this book may have changed since publication and may no longer be valid. The views expressed in this work are solely those of the author and do not necessarily reflect the views of the publisher, and the publisher hereby disclaims any responsibility for them.

ISBN: 978-0-9978157-0-2 (sc)
ISBN: 978-0-9978157-1-9 (e)

Printed in the United States of America.

2Xalt Press rev. date: 14 February 2018

Contents

STAR Leadership Overview.. 1
  STAR Performance Foundation 1
  How to Use this Text 3
Evolution of Leadership Theory 5
  The 1st Paradigm Shift..7
    The 'Great Man' Theory 8
    Theory X...9
    Theory Y..11
    Trait Theory 14
    Contingency Theory 17
  The 2nd Paradigm Shift 17
    Behavioral Theory 18
    Work Maturity Model...19
  The 3rd Paradigm Shift.. 23
    Servant Leadership 24
      What is Servant Leadership? 24
      Being a Servant Leader..34
    STAR Leadership 36
  The Shifts... 38
Leadership at its Core.. 41
  Core Leadership Theory... 42
    The Foundation Postulate 42
    The Service Postulate 44
    The Focus Postulate...44
    The Function Postulate 47
    The Alignment Postulate 48
    The Adaptability Postulate..49
    The Coaching Postulate 50
    Application of Postulates 51
  Core Leadership Ideology 53
    Purpose 53
    Principles..55
      Values..55
      The Seven Pillars of STAR Leadership............................59
    Passion...99
      The Vision Vector™...100
    Persistence..103
Strategic Leadership... 111
Acknowledgements... 119
About the Author 120

Purpose
Principles
Passion
Persistence

STAR Leadership Overview

STAR Performance Foundation

STAR (Strategy, Tactics, Action, Results) Performance™ is a leadership model that unites planning with doing. The STAR Leadership™ model delves even deeper into what makes some leaders great while others quit or quietly fade away. STAR Leadership™ is a proven process that teaches leaders how to be persistent in their actions by learning from and acting upon feedback from results.

The key attributes of STAR Leadership are strategic leadership, tactical leadership, and performance leadership.

Figure 1. STAR Performance

This process begins with the understanding of purpose, which leads to the creation of vision, and the development of plans to solidify it. It requires persistent action and constant response to feedback, and will ultimately lead to the achievement of mission success! When your strategy, tactics, action, and results unite with and focus on your organization's vision, your performance levels will skyrocket!

1

First of all, STAR Performance™ involves "planning" and "doing". The "planning" component is made up of strategy and tactics, and the "doing" component is the action and results.

Strategy is the integration of purpose, principles, and passion. Purpose is at the core of our existence. It is the most fundamental, basic reason for existing. Whether referring to the life of an individual or an organization, purpose is the meaning of life.

Building on our purpose, our principles define the values by which we live. They are the nonnegotiable tenants of operation that we guard dear and which define our character. The fruit of character and integrity are the actions we make when no one is looking. And these actions are determined by our principles.

Finally, we get to passion. Passion is what keeps us going. Without passion we are doomed to failure, but with passion even our failures become more about learning lessons than about weighing us down. Passion is the result of an inspiring vision.

Tactics define the "how". They are the things we do on a daily basis to make progress towards our objectives.

Action is about taking the steps necessary to succeed, and results are the outcomes of this action.

The key attributes of high performance leadership—STAR Leadership™—are strategic leadership, tactical leadership, and performance leadership. This book on strategic leadership is will be the first in the STAR

Leadership™ trilogy covering each of these key attributes.

In this volume we will examine Strategic Leadership. To put STAR Leadership™ into perspective, let's begin with a review of the history and evolution of thought leadership throughout the modern era.

How to Use this Text

This text is designed as a study in the foundational principles of leadership. It is meant to help you improve your understanding of what it means to be a leader and, ultimately, to improve your leadership skills. Its contents will stand alone on their own merit, yet you will get the most out of this book when you combine it with the other volumes to get the full picture of STAR Leadership™.

This text is also the required reading in 2Xalt's STAR Leadership™ certification program, the Martial Art of Leadership. Through this program you can pursue a Green Belt, Brown Belt, and Black Belt in STAR Leadership™. The Green Belt covers the concepts of Strategic Leadership. The Brown Belt applies Tactical Leadership, and the Black Belt helps you gain expertise in Performance Leadership.

I have left a wide margin on the outside edge of each text page within the book. The intent is to provide space for you to take notes and write down ideas that come to you as you read. Occasionally, I have placed a note in this margin space to highlight important points that I believe will be helpful for you to remember.

Enjoy your journey as you explore the principles of strategic leadership under the STAR Leadership™ program.

Evolution of Leadership Theory

Researchers, academics, and popular leadership gurus have different opinions as to what leadership is. Personally, I think they often over think it. Leadership is not about position, or title, or even responsibility. Simply stated, leadership is about influence, or the process or ability to influence the thoughts and actions of others. Peter Northouse said, "Leadership is a process whereby an individual influences a group of individuals to achieve a common goal."[1] Even so, John C. Maxwell succinctly stated that "Leadership is influence. That's it. Nothing more; nothing less."[2]

LEADERSHIP

Influence

Ability

Process

Leadership is the summation of influence, ability, and process. Although, fundamentally, Leadership is influence itself, it is also the ability to generate influence and the process by which influence takes place.

$$Leadership = \sum_{Ability}^{Process} Influence$$

When we strive to lead, we are striving to influence others. Influence is simply molding the thoughts and behaviors of someone else. It is the most basic component of leadership simply because it is the end goal. Our integrity determines our motives behind this desire to influence. For example, selfless motives are based on integrity and will create long-term, passionate followers. Selfish motives may work well in the short-term, but ultimately will not attract loyal followers.

However, leadership is more than just the influence it creates. Leadership is also the ability to generate influence and thus mold the thoughts and behaviors of others. In other words, what is it about you that excites people and causes them to want to follow you? Is it your character, your passion, your persistence? What is it about you that gives you the ability to lead?

In the following sections, we'll review three key paradigm shifts in scholarly thinking on leadership. Some believe that the ability to lead is a birthright—you're either born with it, or you'll never have it. Some believe that the ability to lead is based on measurable traits that are common in all leaders in all situations. Others believe that the ability to lead can be learned and improved upon. Where you fall in this spectrum of leadership thought will determine the effectiveness of your leadership development.

Leadership is also a process. It is the process by which one influences the thoughts and behaviors of others. There are things that good leaders do on a consistent basis. Great leaders do these things extremely well. STAR Leaders™ practice them intentionally and consistently to form a process that inspires people to perform at exceptional levels—even impressing themselves with what they can accomplish.

As you read about the three paradigm shifts in leadership thinking—and the rest of this book on STAR Leadership™ for that matter--keep in mind the definition of leadership as the summation of influence, ability, and process.

The 1st Paradigm Shift

Throughout decades of formal study there have been many theories about leadership. Some of the more prominent theories are important to understand because of their impact on modern leadership theory, and the transformation of theory into workable solution. It is important to review some of these theories because their development and evolution provides a framework for understanding the roots of STAR Leadership.

At the start of the industrial age, leadership was perceived as a 'top down' activity that involved someone in a managerial role assigned too direct, control, and modify the behavior of followers. It was the manager's responsibility to whip the troops into shape and ensure that they performed in the best interest of the organization. Only those born with the traits required for leadership would ever be in such a management role, much less a higher-ranking executive or government official role. This is a holdover from the era of kings and emperors who convinced the masses that only they have the 'divine birthright' to rule. I call this the "Master Birthright" Paradigm, because it reflects the belief that certain individuals are simply born to be the master of others.

It was also a commonly held belief that the average person was either lazy or indifferent, and that he or she lacked the capacity for handling responsibility on his or her own. Then came the first major paradigm shift in thinking on leadership: When Douglas McGregor introduced the concepts of Theory X and Theory Y. As we review these theories--and related theories of organizational leadership—we'll see

Master Birthright Paradigm

Great Man
Leadership is a birthright

Theory X
Followers are naturally lazy and unmotivated and must be forced to be productive

7

a shift from the Master Birthright Paradigm to, what I like to call, the Inheritance Paradigm. This shift marks an incremental change in the perception of what it means to be a leader, with a remarkable change in the perception of followers.

The 'Great Man' Theory

In this theory of leadership, it is assumed that leadership is something with which one is born. It is assumed that great leaders are born, not made, and that great leaders will arise to the occasion where there is a need. A key and early proponent of this theory was Thomas Carlyle, who is quoted as saying, "The history of the world is but the biography of great men."[3]

This theory assumes that what comprises a great leader is provided at birth by divine appointment. There is no consideration of learnable skills or environmental impact. Arguments in favor of this theory point to significant leaders throughout history and presume that they simply rose to the occasion. There is no hint of the possibility that great leaders in history would not have had the possibility of rising to the occasion had they not been influenced by training, experience, and social conditions. These referenced examples "often included aristocratic rulers who achieved their position through birthright. Because people of a lesser social status had fewer opportunities to practice and achieve leadership roles, it contributed to the idea that leadership is an inherent ability."[4]

The biggest problem with the "Great Man Theory" is that it overlooks the potential to learn. Every person on this planet is divinely appointed with a personality, and certain talents and traits. What we do with these traits is entirely up to the individual. If we continually learn and apply them, then we have the potential to lead. We must also be careful not to overlook the fact that leadership comes in a variety of shapes and sizes. Leadership can be cultivated, developed, and instilled. Look at the transformation that takes place in many 18-year-old kids that join the military. Boot camp has a way of transforming a thoughtless teenager into a productive contributor—a leader.

Consider the thoughts of Harvard leadership professor, John Kotter: "The single biggest error in the traditional model is related to its assumptions about the origins of leadership. Stated simply, the historically dominant concept takes leadership skills as a divine gift of birth, a gift granted to a small number of people.... I have found that the traditional idea simply does not fit well with what I have observed in nearly thirty years of studying organizations and the people who run them. In particular, the older model is nearly oblivious to the power and the potential of lifelong learning."[5]

Theory X

Douglas McGregor presented the concepts of *Theory X and Theory Y* leadership in a 1957 paper entitled "The Human Side of Enterprise," published by MIT.[6] A few years later he expanded this paper to a book by the same title.[7]

Prior to this publication, leadership and management were largely held to be synonymous, and this conventional approach believed that the manager's role was to direct, control, and modify the behavior of employees. McGregor called this conventional approach to leadership, 'Theory X' and summarized the Theory X assumptions as follows:[8]

The average human being has an inherent dislike of work and will avoid it if he can.

In other words, the "old school thinking" assumed that people were generally lazy and wouldn't do anything that they didn't feel they had to do.

Most people must be coerced, controlled, directed, threatened with punishment to get them to put forth adequate effort toward the achievement of organizational objectives.

"Theory X" reasoning assumed that micromanagement and a big stick were required to get action from people. No one cared about their work, it was believed, but they cared about themselves; thus, if there were serious repercussions due to underperformance, workers would be sure to put in a good effort.

The average human being prefers to be directed, wishes to avoid responsibility, has relatively little ambition, wants security above all.

These assumptions will obviously lead to a rather dictatorial approach to leadership. Interestingly, McGregor points out that human behavior in the industrial organization of the time, as observed and studied by social scientists, appeared to be precisely what conventional management perceived it to be. He was not arguing against the observations, but rather presenting a case that, perhaps, the observed employee behavior was a result of management's action and attitude, rather than man's inherent nature. He taught that "Theory X is not a straw man for purpose of demolition, but is in fact a theory which materially influences managerial strategy..."[9] (McGregor 35). He knew the behavior to be true and observable, but that opposing observations were equally as true and supported the conclusion that behaviors that seemingly support Theory X assumptions were actually the effect of the assumptions, rather than the cause. He stated that "People, deprived of opportunities to satisfy at work the needs which are now important to them, behave exactly as we might predict—with indolence, passivity, unwillingness to accept responsibility, resistance to change, willingness to follow the demagogue, unreasonable demands for economic benefits. It would seem that we may be caught in a web of our own weaving."

Theory Y

McGregor drew upon the work of his colleague, Abraham Maslow, who published a paper in 1943 describing a hierarchy of human needs, listed in order of fulfillment priority: [1] physiological, [2] safety, [3] love, [4] esteem, and [5] self-actualization (Maslow). Because this hierarchy of needs suggests that people desire to contribute to something bigger than themselves (self-actualization as the fulfillment of potential to contribute to society), but will only be able to do so when their more basic needs are fulfilled first, McGregor suggested what was then a ground-breaking and revolutionary proposal, which he called "Theory Y".

Theory Y presents a new paradigm in initial assumptions about leadership. These assumptions begin with a positive view of human nature and the ability for leadership to occur at all levels. The first assumption of Theory Y is:

The expenditure of physical and mental effort in work is as natural as play or rest[10] (McGregor 47).

This assumption is diametrically opposed to the Theory X assumption of laziness and passivity. It states that work is something that comes naturally to human beings and implies that the proper execution of work—which leads to accomplishment—provides the fulfillment of basic human needs for self-actualization. In fact, it can be said that, from the beginning of time, mankind was meant for work: "The Lord God took the man and put him in the Garden of Eden to *work* it and *keep* it" [emphasis mine].[11]

The second assumption of Theory Y involves the implementation of control and discipline to the work that is being done.

External control and the threat of punishment are not the only means for bringing about effort toward organizational objectives. Man will exercise self-direction and self-control in the service of objectives to which he is committed.[12]

The carrot and stick approach may work at times, but it isn't the only means of motivation available to leaders. In fact, if given a cause that they can believe in--a purpose that they are committed to--people will be self-disciplined and internally motivated.

*Commitment to objectives is a function of
the rewards associated with their
achievement.[13]*

McGregor explains that the rewards here are not necessarily awards provided by management (e.g. monetary, promotional, etc.). The most significant of rewards is actually the fulfillment of the fundamental needs of mankind. The feelings of accomplishment and contribution that result from "satisfaction of ego and self-actualization needs."[14]

*The average human being learns, under
proper conditions, not only to accept, but
to seek responsibility.[15]*

This assumption is based on an understanding of traits, such as the avoidance of responsibility and lack of ambition as the effects not the cause.

*The capacity to exercise a relatively high
degree of imagination, ingenuity, and
creativity in the solution of organizational
problems is widely, not narrowly,
distributed in the population.[16]*

In other words, almost everyone has the ability to contribute to organizational problem solving.

*Under the conditions of modern industrial
life, the intellectual potentialities of the
average human being are only partially
utilized.[17]*

This last assumption is dated; however, the prevalence of 'old paradigm' thinking in today's corporations is shocking. When will we, as leaders, learn that we must provide purpose and inspire passion if we are to create truly high-performance teams?

When will we, as leaders, learn that we must provide purpose and inspire passion if we are to create truly high-performance teams?

Both Theory X and Theory Y define leadership in accordance to the followers, rather than by the leader. In other words, the leadership in each theory is a response to *a priori* assumptions about those that are being led. It doesn't tell us anything about the leaders themselves.

Trait Theory

Like the "Great Man Theory", Trait Theory assumes that leadership traits are inherited rather than learned. The difference is that Trait Theory does not equate this inheritance to some mystical divine appointment that causes the right leader to magically appear when needed. Instead, Trait Theory developed through careful analysis of the characteristics commonly found in leaders and assumed that these characteristics are either present at birth or not.

For instance, it is commonly assumed that great leaders need to be full throttle extroverts to "take command" of a situation or organization. An opinion article in *The New York Times* put it this way: "We prize leaders who are eager talkers over those who have something to say."[18]

However, history teaches that extroversion is not necessarily a good indicator of leadership capability because there have been plenty of great leaders that leaned more toward introversion than extroversion. In an article for *Inc.*, John Rampton lists twenty-three introverts who were strong leaders in their respective fields, including Albert Einstein, Rosa Parks, Bill Gates, Steven Spielberg, Isaac Newton, Mark Zukerberg, Larry Page, Abraham Lincoln, Warren Buffett, Mahatma Gandhi, Elon Musk, and more.[19] I've personally met two of these people, Larry Page and Elon Musk, and from a very brief meeting, in both cases, I would agree that they appeared to be introverts. Yet they also exude incredible passion for what they do, and are clearly driven towards a vision that they hunger to see fulfilled.

In another *Inc.* article, Russ Fujioka, President of Xero US and self-proclaimed introvert, explains that introverted tendencies, such as deep thinking and deliberate speaking, can be advantageous. Furthermore, to be in a leadership seat, he explains that the introvert needs to learn how to "act the part of the extrovert." Mr. Fujioka quotes another introverted leader, Bill Gates: "If you're clever, you can learn to get the benefits of being an introvert, which might be, say, being willing to go off for a few days and think about a tough problem, read everything you can, push yourself very hard to think out on the edge of that area. Then, if you come up with something, if you want to hire people, get them excited, build a company around that idea, you better learn what extroverts do, you better hire some extroverts...."[20]

Another study performed by researchers at University of Pennsylvania's Wharton School, Harvard Business School, and Kenan-Flagler Business School [UNC] found that neither introversion, nor extroversion, had a universal advantage for leadership. Rather, there were certain situations in which introversion was an advantage and other situations in which extroversion was more effective.[21] They found that neither introversion, or extroversion, provided a universally greater leadership quality. In fact, the discovery is that organizations, and the people that define them, are complex. So much so, that no one personality can ever be defined as superior, or always more effective, with regards to organizational leadership.[22] In other words, the most effective leadership style varies depending on the makeup of the team.

Psychologist Kendra Cherry stated that "Early studies on leadership focused on the differences between leaders and followers with the assumption that people in leadership positions would display more 'leadership traits' than those in subordinate positions. What researchers found, however, was that there were relatively few traits that could be used to distinguish between leaders and followers." She referenced multiple studies that suggest that leadership is not the result of predefined traits, but that the traits of leaders varies depending on the situation.[23]

The bottom line is that research clearly indicates that no specific set of traits is universally applicable, or required, for leadership. Rather, different traits have different values at different times and in different situations.

Inheritance Paradigm

Theory Y
Follows desire to perform, but basic needs must be met first

Trait Theory
Leaders are born with traits to lead

Contingency
Ideal traits, and thus ideal leaders, vary by situation

Contingency Theory

This evidence and line of reasoning leads us to the 'Contingency Theory', which assumes that no leadership style or trait is universally ideal. One style or accumulation of traits may work well in a given situation, and yet be completely inadequate in a different situation. This model was championed by management psychologist Fred Fielder who recognized the variability in styles needed in different scenarios.

Contingency Theory also assumes that individuals have a fixed set of traits available to them; therefore, no individual is generally capable of consistent leadership. Because leadership traits are assumed to be inherited, if a situation requires different traits, or a different style, the leader must be replaced with another who more closely resembles the traits needed for that situation. In other words, "Fielder's Theory seems to lack flexibility; he believed that we, as leaders, are naturally fixed in how we handle situations and that if we want to change how the situation is handled, we have to change the leader."[24]

The 2nd Paradigm Shift

The first paradigm shift involved a transformation in the perception of people where leaders viewed themselves as an elite few, blessed with ambition, drive, and a desire for responsibility whereas most people were considered lazy, disinterested, and lacking in ambition. However, during the second paradigm shift, the perception that drive, ambition, and desire to take responsibility became far more common place and somewhat universal. Still, the assumption that leaders "are born not made" remained intact, although softened from the "birthright" view to a view that inherited leadership traits are more widely dispersed within the population. Some theories have even suggested that leadership is more broad and inclusive in that what makes for a good leader in one situation is not necessarily going to be a good fit for another. Still, the assumption remains that leadership is an inherited characteristic.

In this second paradigm shift, we'll see a shift from this 'Inheritance Paradigm' to an understanding of leadership as a collection of behaviors rather than traits. I call this the 'Behavior Paradigm.'

Behavioral Theory

The behavioral model jumps to the opposite end of the spectrum. It begins with the assumption that any leadership style is simply the application of learnable behaviors and that people can learn to behave like leaders.

Where prior models have focused on leadership traits, the behavioral model focuses on the actions or behaviors of leaders. Within the behavioral model, there are two style orientations: [1] task-oriented, and [2] relationship-oriented. The task-oriented style is autocratic in nature, the behaviors demonstrated including allocating tasks, setting deadlines, giving direction, etc.

Relationship-oriented style is democratic in nature, and behaviors might include communication, approachability, encouraging participation, etc.

Likert's Management System

Task Oriented
Exploitive Authoritative

Benevolent Authoritative

Relationship Oriented
Consultative Leadership

Participative Leadership

These two orientations were further broken down into four systems by Rensis Likert.[25] These systems are known as Likert's management systems:[26]

- **Exploitive Authoritative:** Based on fear and threats; one-way communication; decision making is centralized

- **Benevolent Authoritative:** Based on rewards; one-way communication; decision-making is centralized

- **Consultative Leadership:** Based on appropriate rewards; two-way communication (limited upwards communication); decision making is decentralized (limited)

- **Participative Leadership:** Based on group participation; two-way communication; decision making is decentralized

This model opened the door to the possibility that leadership skills could be developed over time. Some people may naturally pick up certain skills more easily than others, but the "sandbox" was no longer closed to those not deemed as having the leadership birthright.

Work Maturity Model

The *Work Maturity Model*, also known as the *situational model*, was developed by Paul Hersey and Ken Blanchard.[27] Like the Contingency Theory, the Situational Model assumes that no single leadership style fits all situations. This model suggests that the leader

Situational
Leadership

Directing

Coaching

Supporting

Delegating

has the ability, and even the responsibility, to adapt his or her leadership style based on the maturity of the follower. This situational model "proposes that leadership style should differ based on the subordinates' task maturity (i.e., their existing knowledge and skills) and their psychological maturity (i.e., their ability and confidence). Where maturity is high, the leader can engage in a more participative style than if maturity is low (where a more directive style is needed)."[28]

Because every leader needs to offer various leadership styles based on the situation, leaders must learn and develop those styles that don't come naturally. Thus, situational leadership is a contingency-behavioral hybrid model that draws the most relevant components of each.

Situational leadership assumes that four basic leadership styles are available to every leader: Directing, coaching, supporting, and delegating styles.[29] Each style is basically defined by a varying composition of directive (autocratic or authoritative) behavior, and supportive (democratic or participative) behavior.

The 'directing style' is highly autocratic in that the leader provides specific direction and closely monitors progress. In other words, "You tell the person what the goal is and what a good job looks like, but you also lay out a step-by-step plan about how the task is to be accomplished. You solve the problem. You make the decisions; the person carries out your ideas."[30] In a crisis, where decisions must be made at a very rapid pace, this is a very effective style to use. Think about first responders pulling the injured from a traffic accident or burning building. They need to act immediately; pausing to take input from the team could result in a catastrophic waste of time. Inexperience may also be another situation highly suited for the directive style. When leading people that are inexperienced for the role, it may be necessary to be highly directive to help them learn the ropes. As they mature, or gain experience, the level of direction provided can decrease.

The 'coaching style' still utilizes directive behavior, but also utilizes some supportive behavior. While the leader continues to direct and monitor, he or she will also provide greater explanations of decisions, solicit suggestions, and support progress.[31] This style is used in cases where an inexperienced team member is gaining experience and confidence in his or her ability to perform the role. Gradually transitioning from fully directive, utilizing more and more supportive behaviors is an extremely effective way to transition people into new roles and responsibilities.

It may also be a useful style when more experienced team members face disillusionment or begin to lack confidence for one reason or another. Failing a task is part of the process of learning, but it can also lead to disillusionment if not handled carefully. We want our team members to learn from mistakes, rather than be disillusioned by them. Stepping back from a supporting style to a coaching style that offers a little more directive behavior can be an effective tool for guiding a team member through disillusionment and back to confidence.[32] As a word of caution, I would simply say that care must be taken to ensure that you, as the leader, provide coaching that guides rather than resorting to total directive behavior that can squash innovation.

The supporting style further reduces the ratio of directive behavior to supportive behavior to the point that primarily supportive behavior is utilized. In the words of the "One Minute Manager", you "support your people's efforts, listen to their suggestions, and facilitate their interactions with others. And to build up their confidence and motivation, you encourage and praise."[33] This style of leadership is highly democratic, or participative, in that those being led tend to be highly participative in the decision-making processes. This leadership style works best with experienced and capable team members, and it allows the leader and the organization to benefit from the expertise, talents, and skills of these experienced team members. An ideal team will be dominated by members with appropriate skill and experience to be led with a supportive style.

Less experienced team members are likely to be overwhelmed with the responsibility and unnecessary failure is likely. Rather than doom someone to failure from the beginning, start off with more directive behavior and gradually replace directive behavior with supportive behavior. Only a relatively small percentage of the total makeup of the team should be at such inexperienced stages so as to ensure consistent growth and development of each individual, the team as a whole, and the entire organization being served.

The 'delegating style' leans even further towards supporting behavior, almost entirely in fact. "In [the delegating style], you are turning

Behavioral
Paradigm

Behavioral
Theory
Leadership is
determined by
behavior, rather
than traits

Behavior can be
learned and
modified

Work Maturity
Leadership
behavior must
adapt to the
situation or
experience level
of the follower

22

over responsibility for day-to-day decision-making and problem-solving to the person doing the task."[34] This style will be reserved for the most experienced team members because it effectively grooms them to step up to more senior leadership roles in time. As noted previously, an ideal team consists mostly of experienced people who require a supportive leadership style, and a few people in more of an "apprentice" role that will require a directive style. This ideal team will also have a small percentage of experts needing only a delegating style. In fact, you should be able to delegate some of the leadership of other team members to these individuals. You are likely to find that with any given individual, you can delegate certain tasks while other tasks require more direction. This is a normal part of the leadership process and should be embraced as a means of developing those that you lead.

The 3rd Paradigm Shift

In the first paradigm shift, we saw a transformation in how the masses are perceived. This was a shift from the Master Birthright Paradigm to the Inheritance Paradigm. In the second paradigm shift, we saw a transformation in assumptions about how leadership behaviors are developed (as opposed to inherited). This shift led to the Behavioral Paradigm of organizational leadership theory. In the third paradigm shift, we see a change in the purpose of leadership. I call this that 'STAR Paradigm' because it flows through servant leadership and culminates with the STAR Leadership™ model.

Servant Leadership

The term 'servant leader' was coined by Robert Greenleaf who stated [servant leadership] "begins with the natural feeling that one wants to serve, to serve first. Then the conscious choice brings one to aspire to lead."[35] Yet, the concept of servant leadership is far older than Mr. Greenleaf's writings. In the early first century AD, Jesus taught His disciples that leaders must behave as servants.[36] A half-century earlier (c. 500 BC), Lao Tzu is quoted as saying "the highest type of ruler is one of whose existence the people are barely aware.... The Sage is self-effacing and scanty of words. When his task is accomplished, and things have been completed, all the people say, *We ourselves have achieved it!*"[37]

What is Servant Leadership?

The concept of servant leadership is often misunderstood. As a result, it tends to be overlooked or even held in contempt. When people hear the term "servant", they often equate it with slavery. However, this isn't the intent of the idea of servant leadership.

People who may find the term "servant leadership" distasteful or offensive envision a leader who has been browbeaten and overrun by a team or organization with no discipline bent on forcing its will upon the hierarchy. But doing so, paints a picture of anarchy where the supposed leader is just there to fetch coffee for the team. I, too, would cringe with that kind of leadership image, but that is not what servant leadership is.

Rather than conjuring up such visuals of slave labor and anarchy, allow yourself to see a servant simply as one who serves. The question then becomes whom or what is the servant leader serving. There are many different interpretations and definitions available in literature today. My definition for servant leadership is quite simple: A servant leader is one who leads in order to serve—having a heart to serve—to make a positive difference. Service, then, is the primary motivator of the leader to serve the cause, the organization, the team, and, lastly, individuals.

Some interpret the concept of servant leadership in reverse priority, with the servant leader being first a servant to the individual. I do not believe that this is a proper understanding of true servant leadership. Of course, the servant leader desires the best for each individual and will work hard to enable each individual to succeed. However, there are times when a individual is not in the right role, is not a good fit for the team, or doesn't have the character needed to be part of any team. In some cases, it is simply necessary to sacrifice the needs of an individual for the greater good of the team or the cause. In such cases, the needs of the team must come before the needs of the individual. Consider the infamous words of Mr. Spock, "The needs of the many outweigh the needs of the one."[38]

With this priority of service in mind, realize that the servant leader desires to serve individuals by empowering them to be all that they can and desire to be. The servant leader serves individuals by working to ensure they have the resources needed to optimize performance and satisfaction, and the freedom to use their experience, ingenuity, and logic to think beyond the ordinary, often beyond expectation, as they serve the cause. The servant leader combines a strong focus on results—achievement of objectives in service to the cause with a strong focus on social skills—and service to the individuals that make up the team and organization.

In an article in the *Harvard Business Review*, Matthew Lieberman discusses the relative importance of a results focus or a people focus. In this article, he shares research showing that "results oriented" people were seen as great leaders by 14% of 60,000 employees surveyed, and those with strong social skills were only perceived as great leaders by 12% of the people. The "ah-ha" moment comes when considering leaders with both a strong focus on results and good people skills. Mr. Lieberman notes that in "leaders who were strong in both results focus and in social skills, the likelihood of being seen as a great leader skyrocketed to 72%."[39] The reality, though, is that most bosses aren't like this. Furthermore, Mr. Lieberman shares additional research indicating that less than 1% of business leaders have a strong focus on both results and people. The truth is that most people are naturally drawn to either a results focus or a people focus. Very rarely (if ever) does one individual have a natural talent for both. Additionally, Mr. Lieberman states that when we are actively focused on results, our ability to focus on people is diminished—and vice versa. This isn't opinion, guesswork, or hearsay. It is scientifically quantifiable and verifiable fact that Mr. Lieberman refers to as the *neural seesaw*.[40]

What does this mean for the servant leader? It means that to be great leaders, we must develop both a strong focus on results *and* good social skills that allow strong communication, conflict resolution, and a sensitivity to concerns or social impediments to high team performance. We aren't likely to be naturally strong in both areas, so we need to be extremely intentional at developing skills and proactively putting them into action.

Having defined whom and what the servant leader serves, let's consider why the servant leader serves. For some, leadership is about a drive for power and authority. For others, leadership is about higher pay and material possessions. For the servant leader, leadership is a process for service and the accomplishment of an objective. Leadership is not the objective itself. Because the servant leader serves a cause, there is a passion to see the cause become a reality. This results in a need to rally support for the accomplishment of the cause, which eventually takes the form of an organization and teams comprised of individuals.

When a leader's motivation is fueled by a desire to serve a cause—and a desire to serve those that show a similar passion for the cause—the behavior of the leader will be different. The Blanchard Management Corporation teaches that "The most persistent barrier to being a servant leader is a heart motivated by self-interest that looks at the world as a "give a little, take a lot" proposition. Leaders with a heart motivated by self-interest put their own agenda, safety, status, and gratification ahead of those affected by their thoughts and actions."[41] (Servant Leadership 258-259).

To illustrate, let's consider how several different teams—each working independently—might tackle the same project: A low-cost, lightweight, easily deployable modular unit that uses renewable energy to power a system that pumps water from a well and filters it for safe human consumption. For the sake of this discussion, let's assume that these teams are identical in every way—except for their leadership.

Team One

The first team has a passionate leader that is highly results-oriented. He believes in the cause and won't let anything or anyone deter progress towards the project's completion. He drives the team hard—hammering them with the importance of the cause and reminds them how many children are dying in third world countries because they don't have access to clean drinking water. The team buys into the cause and goes along with the demands by working 80-hour weeks for months as the project moves along.

The exhausted mechanical engineer is growing frustrated with the software developer and makes several comments to others on the team about how the software developer isn't producing. Meanwhile, the software developer is burning the midnight oil trying to work the bugs out of the code so that it will do what it's intended to do. However, the long working hours are taking their toll, and the software developer is often putting as many new bugs into the code as he is taking them out.

The results-oriented leader is so focused on driving the team that he doesn't notice how exhausted the team members are becoming. He isn't receptive to the brewing conflicts that are hampering their current progress and are about to escalate when the team brings its individual contributions together as a unit working toward an integrated solution.

This team will eventually complete the design and get the solution built. But it will likely take longer than anticipated. The quality of the solution may be adequate, but it won't be exceptional.

Team Two

The second team has a leader that is intent on making sure every team member has solid input on the design, that all ideas are discussed and considered, and that everyone is continually supporting one another. She also drives the team hard, reminding everyone of the importance of their mission: To provide safe drinking water for third world countries.

Because of their passion for the cause, the team is working 80-hour weeks for months on end. Several months into the project, they are getting along with one another quite nicely, but seem to get hung up on deliberation and discussion in efforts to achieve consensus, so much so that actual progress is slow.

The electrical engineer starts expressing frustration in muffled comments to herself but not loud enough for anyone to hear. However, the leader senses the engineer's frustration—due to her body language—and holds a meeting with the team to discuss her issues and concerns. The team spends the next hour talking through their concerns with one another, and, at the end of the discussion, they are once again supportive of one another—yet little progress has been achieved for the day.

Ultimately, Team Two completes the design. Even though their finished solution has a few more ideas and concepts—some being legitimate improvements while others are merely included to make a team member feel better—the timeline and project cost is remarkably similar to Team One's.

Team Three

The leader of the third team has a high level of passion for the project, has a natural results-oriented focus, and is very intentional about proactively observing and responding to the human needs of team members. This leader emphasizes the importance of the mission, much the same as the first two leaders. During the presentation of the mission, this leader talks about budget constraints, critical deadlines, specific applications where the end product is expected to be used, and the difference that the solution will make in the quality of life for those that utilize it. The team is energized and would eagerly put in 80+ hour work weeks, but the leader is careful to limit their workload. Although the team's enthusiasm for working long hours is tempting, this leader is keenly aware of the diminishing returns that result from working long hours over an extended period of time. He makes it clear to the team that their enthusiasm is greatly appreciated, but that he wants them to return to work refreshed and mentally recharged the next day. He emphasizes the importance of them spending time with their families, recognizing that their families may also share in the passion they feel for this mission rather than harboring resentments for working long hours. As a result, he will encourage those 80-hour work weeks only in emergency situations, and he has made it clear to team members that they won't be allowed to work long hours for more than a couple of weeks at a time. In doing so, the team members spend time thinking about the designs when they are off-the-clock anyway.

During a design review, every member of this team is encouraged to provide input and every idea is given consideration. However, the leader does not necessarily wait for consensus. Knowing that a decision must be made in order to progress, the leader leaves an appropriate amount of time for discussion and then makes a decision that gives the team direction for the next steps in the project. During this discussion, the leader notices that the software developer said he had an epiphany about how to fix the bugs in the code while taking a shower that morning. The mechanical engineer's nine-year-old thought of a great idea while working on a school project, and the engineer is working on incorporating it into their frame design as a way to reduce weight. The electrical engineer noted that she got an idea for how to reduce manufacturing costs in the circuitry while coaching her child's middle school robotics team over the weekend.

Midway through the project, one of the major investors takes exception to procurement's supplier choices. (The procurement person had developed fairly tight supplier requirements that were designed to reduce cost and ensure inventory availability.

These procedures had resulted in a change in battery suppliers, the offended investor having owned a large stake in the battery supplier that had been eliminated). The investor ordered the leader to terminate the procurement person, revise the policies, and reinstate the battery supplier immediately or he would no longer invest in the project. The leader knew that the procurement officer's actions were justified but he also realized that losing the funds from this investor would be detrimental to the project. The leader also knew that this investor could use his influence on the board to remove him from the project.

Despite these risks, the leader stood by the procurement officer and refused to meet the investor's demands. He proactively communicated what had happened to the other board members and shared his plan to replace the funding if it was lost. Everyone on the team recognized the risk that the leader took by supporting the procurement officer, which only strengthened their loyalty to him. In the end, this distraction proved to be minor and the project continued forward. The offended investor did back out, and alternate sources of funding were utilized. However, this same investor pressured the battery supplier he owned equity in to improve their process. Ultimately they did so, and were eventually reinstated as a supplier for this project. This leader's willingness to take a stand helped two companies improve.

Towards the end of development, the team worked an 85-hour week, followed by a 100-hour week—after which the team is exhausted, but the solution is ready to ship. The project is completed in less than half of the time that it took the first two teams, and the end result is 15% lighter and will produce 50% more drinking water in a 24-hour period. The first Monday after the solution ships, the leader caters a celebratory brunch and gives everyone the rest of the week off as a thank you for their efforts. A few days later, each team member's spouse receives a handwritten thank you note from the leader, and, without any fanfare, a sizeable bonus appears on the team members' next paychecks.

Why are the results better for this third team? It isn't because they had more passion for the cause, or because they just worked harder, or even because they had better fitting personalities, or stronger talent. As a matter of fact, all three teams were identical—having the same interpersonal relationships and personalities, the same passion for the cause, the same talent and skill, and the same work ethic. The difference was the leadership. The leader of the first team was so focused on results that he missed many interpersonal issues that killed efficiency. The leader of the second team was so focused on interpersonal interactions that she missed deadlines and didn't keep the team effectively on target, which had a similar effect on the team's efficiency. The leader of the third team balanced a focus on results with proactive and intentional efforts to manage relationships, individual contributions, and the health and well-being of the team members. This resulted in a team filled with leaders, who, being well rested and sharp, were highly creative in providing innovative solutions, all the while being constantly aware of the schedule.

A 12-step program to becoming a servant leader doesn't really exist. In fact, servant leadership is really a matter of heart, attitude, and motives as opposed to action. But, when the heart, attitude, and motive of servant leadership is present then actions will follow.

The heart of a servant leader is passionate about purpose, and it recognizes the value of every individual contributor to that purpose. The leader will find ways to make sure all contributors understand the value they bring to the team (and, more importantly, the value the leader sees in them). Colin Powell is an excellent example of a great modern-day leader. He entered the United States Army, as a second lieutenant, in 1958 after receiving his BS degree in Geology from the City College of New York where he was enrolled in the ROTC. In 1979, he became a general with the award of his first star (Brigadier General) and has since served this country as National Security Advisor for President Ronald Reagan, Commander of the U.S. Army Forces Command, Chairman of the Joint Chiefs of Staff under Presidents George H.W. Bush and Bill Clinton, and Secretary of State under George W. Bush. He was the first African-American to serve on the Joint Chiefs of Staff and the first African-American to serve as Secretary of State. Clearly, Mr. Powell is a highly accomplished leader, who has demonstrated a strong focus on both results and people and linking them both to purpose.[42]

On the topic of purpose, Mr. Powell says that "Leaders must embed their own sense of purpose into the heart and soul of every follower…. Great leaders inspire every follower at every level to internalize their purpose, and to understand that their purpose goes far beyond the mere details of their job."[43] It is the leader's responsibility to communicate the purpose, or cause, to the team and to inspire each individual team member to adopt this purpose as his or her own.

Regarding results, Mr. Powell states, "To achieve his purpose, a successful leader must set demanding standards and make sure they are met." A strong, results driven approach, it is also an admission that if high standards are to be met, they first must be set. And setting the standards isn't enough. There also must be a strong sense of accountability to those standards.

In addition, Mr. Powell also demonstrated a strong focus on people. Not only did he recognize the need to help every team member personally adopt the purpose, he also knew how important each team member was to the standards. "Standards must be achievable (though achieving them will always require extra effort), **and the leaders must provide the means to get there**" [emphasis mine].[44] The leader is a servant to the team in the sense that he or she is responsible for providing the means to achieve the objectives. Powell also said that "everything you do as a leader has to focus on building trust in a team. Trust among the leaders, trust among the followers, and trust between the leaders and the followers. **And it begins with selfless, trusting leaders**" [emphasis mine].[45] For a leader to be able to build a team where members trust one another, he or she must first demonstrate his or her own trustworthiness, and trust for the team. This requires the selfless action of a servant leader.

STAR Leadership

When strategy, tactics, action, and results are focused on a common target, the result is always higher performance.[46] STAR Leadership™ extends this understanding to the principles of leadership by recognizing the three major elements of leadership as strategic leadership, tactical leadership, and performance leadership (a combination of action and results)—ensuring that all three elements of leadership must have a common focus.

Figure 2 STAR Leadership Pyramid™

As illustrated in the STAR Leadership Pyramid™, strategic leadership provides the foundation for tactical and performance leadership. Because it is the foundation, it is critically important. Yet the majority of a leader's time should be invested in the tactical and performance elements of leadership.

Strategic leadership has two sub-elements: Theory and ideology. The theory element is the

Core Leadership Theory (CLT) that defines the leader's worldview. This is how the leader sees others, defines expectations, and determines how leader/follower interaction will take place. The ideology element is defined by the Four Ps of Strategic Leadership: Purpose, Principles, Passion, and Persistence.

Tactical Leadership defines how a leader leads. It involves an omnidirectional leadership focus, an agile and adaptable leadership style, the intentional application of key leadership practices, and a commitment to leadership development through lifelong learning. (Tactical leadership will be discussed in greater detail in the second book in the STAR Leadership™ trilogy).

Performance Leadership is about taking action and getting results. It involves the daily alignment of the operations and the organizational structure to the vision and purpose as well as a focus on continual improvement.

The STAR Leader™—in each of the above-mentioned elements of leadership—is motivated first to serve the cause, then, in the following order, the organization, the team, and the individuals. A STAR Leader™ recognizes that the people on his or her team are its most valuable asset, and thus empowers them to think creatively and to lead themselves—all the while fully supporting them in their decisions.

If a team member is not supportive of the cause or the team, the STAR Leader™ decisively solves this issue by either understanding and addressing the team member's concerns or removing that individual

STAR Paradigm

Ideal leadership
requires keen
focus on both
results &
relationships.

Ideal leadership
flows from desire
to serve.

Leadership is a
function of
behavior.

Leadership
consists of three
fundamental
elements:

Strategic
Leadership

Tactical
Leadership

Performance
Leadership

from the team. When team members are passionate about the cause and are acting in service to the team, the STAR Leader™ empowers them by coaching them, delegating to them as appropriate, and defending them with passion and gusto. If such a valuable and supportive team member makes a mistake, the STAR Leader™ doesn't place blame. Rather, the leader accepts the blame and helps solve the problem. If necessary, the leader then coaches the team member to learn from the experience to minimize the risk of recurrence. If appropriate, the STAR Leader™ works with the team member to create, or modify, processes and procedures in accordance with the lessons learned. As Collin Powell states very simply, "Share the credit, take the blame, and quietly find out and fix things that went wrong."[47] Moreover, Rudy Giuliani observes that "leaders who stand by their employees, even those who make mistakes, can enjoy the benefits of hiring the absolute best person for the job."[48]

The Shifts

As stated previously, three key paradigm shifts have taken place in organizational leadership theory:

- The first is the shift from the "Master Birthright Paradigm" to the "Inheritance Paradigm."

- The second is from the "Inheritance" to the "Behavior Paradigm."

- The third being from behaviors to STARs, specifically into the "STAR Paradigm."

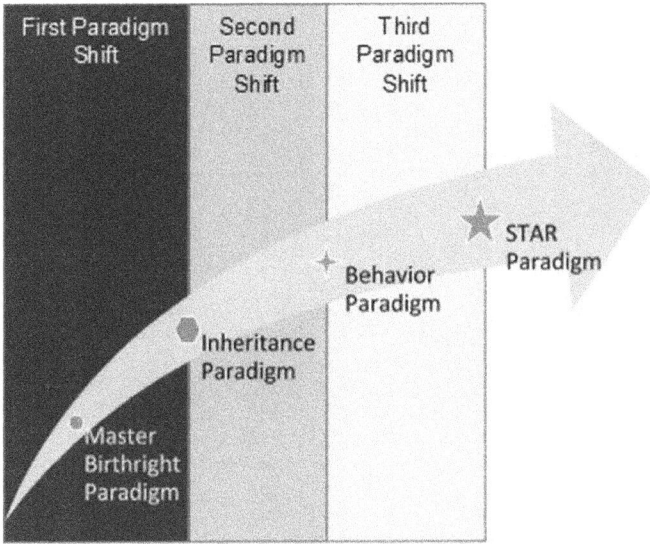

Figure 3 Three Paradigm Shifts

Leadership at its Core

As we noted in the previous chapter, ideal leadership requires a keen focus on both results and relationships. You simply cannot sustain one without the other over the long term. We also now understand that leadership is a function of behavior. Ideal leadership, therefore, results from behavior that simultaneously builds relationships and drives results.

Furthermore, ideal leadership, and the behavior from which it results, stems from a desire to serve. This heart for service begins with a purpose and extends to the people that also share a passion for that purpose.

These key points form the basis of the core doctrine of STAR Leadership™. A core doctrine consists of a combination of Core Leadership Theory (CLT) and Core Leadership Ideology (CLI). Strategic leadership in this context is simply the application of the core doctrine of STAR Leadership™ in a manner that is both meaningful and productive.

The theory portion of strategic leadership is foundational because it determines the leader's perspective or worldview. It isn't necessarily something that a leader communicates or talks about with followers, but the followers will recognize and understand the leader's CLT by the actions and behaviors that the leader exhibits.

The ideology portion of strategic leadership is also foundational because it defines the fundamental cause for the team, the values that

Ideal leadership results from behavior that simultaneously builds relationships and drives results.

41

govern the team, and the vision for the future that inspires the team.

Core Leadership Theory

The Core Leadership Theory (CLT) is the perspective, or worldview, through which leaders conduct themselves. Your perspective on leadership is your CLT, and it will determine the behaviors that you exhibit in the course of providing leadership in any context.

For example, leaders that ascribe to the "Great Man" theory consider themselves to be of the ruling class, and everyone else is a minion who carries out their bidding.

Leaders with a "Theory X" mentality assume that all team members are lazy and refuse to accept responsibility voluntarily. They will be harsh and forceful with their teams because they believe this is the only way to get results.

Leaders who adopt a "Theory Y" perspective believe that people want to contribute and accept responsibility but must first have their most basic needs met.

But, the CLT of STAR Leadership™ is built upon a series of seven postulates about the leader, the followers, and the cause: Foundation, Service, Focus, Function, Alignment, Adaptability, and Coaching.

The Foundation Postulate

STAR Leadership™ requires a common focus on a worthy cause, rock solid values, and an inspiring vision. Having this common focus can only happen when these elements are clearly defined and continually communicated. These elements are drawn directly from the "Three Ps of Strategy": Purpose, Principles, and Passion.

Your purpose is the cause that you serve. If your cause is worthy, it will attract followers. If it isn't, perhaps you should rethink what your purpose should be. Because purpose finds its way into every aspect of leadership, we'll investigate it in depth in the section on ideology.

Your principles are your values. If they are shifty and shaky, you won't generate trust from those you lead. However, if they are firm, you will gain the trust of those around you. Some may disagree with your values, and may not follow. That's OK—you wouldn't want them on your team anyway. It's nothing personal. Rather, if they don't agree with and accept the principles driving the organization, they will inevitably derail efforts and hold back progress. On the other hand, if they do believe in and accept the principles, maintaining the principles will not be a chore. In fact, you're likely to find that they will hold you accountable if you step beyond the principles (which is exactly what you want from your team).

Passion comes from an inspiring vision. It's not enough to have a strong sense of purpose with which people agree, or to have solid principles that govern decisions and behaviors. You simply must have a vision for the future that makes your purpose and principles meaningful. When this vision is inspiring, you get passion, and it is passion which drives results.

The Service Postulate

STAR Leaders™ are called to serve a higher purpose, and to have a willing heart to serve those that share in this calling.

In serving a purpose, STAR Leaders™ serve the organizations for which they work, serve the teams which they lead, and serve the individuals which comprise those teams.

The Focus Postulate

STAR Leaders™ focus heavily on both results and relationships—specifically relationships among people who make those results possible. They care as deeply about the people on their team as they do about the cause that they serve.

The focus on results is what drives short-term success. To have a winning team, there must be a strong focus on winning the game (i.e. short term success).

The focus on relationships enables the long-term sustainment of success. To be a 'legacy team' there must be a strong relationship that binds the team together and keeps them passionately focused on improving results.

Consider Super Bowl winning NFL teams. Obviously, a team doesn't get to the Super Bowl, much less win it, without a keen focus on results. There have been several teams that have won once, but then have fallen apart during the following seasons—sometimes not even making the playoffs the season after winning it all. In fact, nearly a third of all winning Super Bowl teams didn't make the playoffs in the next season. A few, however, have had a string of successful seasons back to back.

For instance, under the leadership of Chuck Noll, the Pittsburg Steelers created a legacy of winning in the 1970s and 80s. When Chuck Noll became the head coach in 1969, he recruited players like Terry Bradshaw, Mel Blount, Jack Ham, Franco Harris, and Joe Green. They won nine Divisional Championships, four AFC titles, and four Super Bowls—with two back-to-back pairs of Super Bowl championships.[49] In 1979 [Super Bowl XIII], they became the first NFL team to win three Super Bowls and then repeated their victory in 1980 [Super Bowl XIV] to become the first team to win four Super Bowls.[50]

Coach Noll had a focus on results, but he also had a focus on building relationships that held the team together. They supported one another, encouraged one another, and held one another accountable. Ultimately, they won a lot of games and had the most championships of any team in their day.

Here is what some of those star players had to say about their coach. John Stallworth said, "I think he deeply considered what I was feeling and what I was going through, and he tried his best to make that easy. That made the relationship special. He had 40, 50, 60 players to deal with, but I always thought he was knowledgeable and considerate of what was going on in the life of John Stallworth." Joe Green: "I watched him, and I saw him show his appreciation for his players and for his team in a very quiet and subtle way." Jack Ham: "He was the glue. He was the guy that got all of us to buy into how to win a championship." Dick

Hoak: "He had everything prioritized right. Your family was first. Take care of your family. And the football came after that. If there was something wrong in your family, you took care of that." Lynn Swann: "He showed us how to live well, and he gave us a foundation that would help us become successful way beyond football." Donnie Shell: "He always took the back seat. He always labored behind the scenes quietly. And that was a great example of a servant leader." [51]

This focus on relationships also requires an understanding of the hierarchy of needs for each individual. Adpated from Maslow's description, this hierarchy of needs begins with the most basic need for survival. [52] Food, water, air to breathe, sufficient sleep, and general good health are all basic survival needs that must be met before anyone can be expected to perform at any level. The next level of need is that of security. To be secure, people need to feel safe, have a sense of stability, and understand the structure in which they must perform. If team members don't feel secure, they will most likely look for a new team. Additonally, people have social needs for friendship, love, and intimacy. Your team needs to experience a bond of friendship. If an individual feels socially disconnected from the team, he or she may accept his or her job but will most likely not feel passionate about it.

Beyond these basic needs for survival, security, and socialization, people need to be esteemed. That is, they need to feel respected, accepted, and valued by their peers and their leaders. When team members feel esteemed, they enjoy their role and become strong performers.

In the diagram below, the pentacle is self-actualization. This is the fulfillment or accomplishment of one's full potential. When an individual's need for self-actualization is met, he or she displays maximum creativity, ingenuity, and self-expression. This helps the individual to grow and develop, enabling him or her to become an outstanding problem solver. Team members can not reach self-actualization unless and until the need for esteem is met. When they do reach self-actualization, they not only become highly engaged team members that enjoy their roles, but also team members that take ownership. These are the qualities that STAR Leaders and STAR Performers possess.

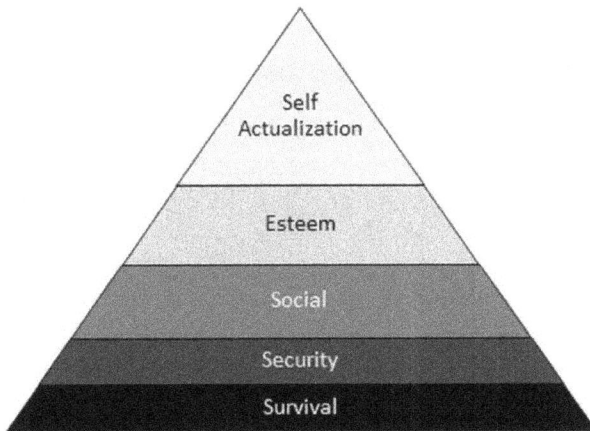

Figure 4. Modified Maslow's Hierarchy of Needs

The Function Postulate

Leadership is a function of behaviors. Good behavior requires skill, and skills can and should be developed. STAR Leaders™ recognize this and are intentional about developing and applying skills in themselves and in those that they lead.

Every leader has a set of God-given natural talents with which to work. These natural talents can be developed and improved, refining them into skills that empower sound behaviors. While skills developed from natural talent often come easily, perfecting them requires practice and correction.

Additionally, leaders can also develop skills in areas that don't necessarily come naturally to themselves.   This will require intentional planning and action, and will ultimately provide a return when it results in improved behaviors that better build relationships and drive results.

The Alignment Postulate

Followers generally have a natural desire to contribute to a greater purpose. This desire is as natural as breathing—it simply requires some enabling for it to manifest.

STAR Leaders™ must find alignment between the cause, or greater purpose, and the vision that inspires the followers. If no alignment can be made, there is either a problem with the vision or with the purpose.

There must also be alignment between the organizational structure and the ideology (purpose, principles, and passion inspiring vision). If the roles and responsibilities don't align with the purpose and vision, how can the organization perform at a higher level? If your compensation plans unintentionally favor violating principles in order to perform, what kind of performance are you encouraging?

Similarly, there must be alignment between the operations and the ideology. When operational processes and procedures are not in alignment with purpose and vision, inefficiencies will result, at best. In some cases, the misalignment may actually result in such poor performance that opportunities are missed and clients are lost.

The challenge for the leader is to recognize that while this postulate freely applies to most people, there will be exceptions. There are those in society (both leaders and followers) whose root desire is to take more than they give, and therefore no amount of alignment will help. These are people you'll want to remove from your team because they will bring down the entire team.

The Adaptability Postulate

STAR Leaders™ exhibit behavioral adaptability in response to the status of their followers' experience and expertise, as well as the status of priority for a given task and the associated risk tolerance.

Every follower has varying levels of experience and expertise, and leaders will need to adapt their style in response to these levels.

Environmental conditions that impact urgency and importance may also require leaders to adapt how they lead in the short term.

Finally, the risk tolerance is an important factor that must drive behavior. In general, we should leave room for failure. Failure is a necessary stepping stone to success, and those that we lead will learn from their mistakes. When possible, we should relay lessons learned from past mistakes so that those we lead have opportunity to learn from our mistakes. However, if we as leaders don't tolerate any mistakes, our followers will never learn and grow. But there are times when failure really isn't an option. Use common sense and don't allow those that you lead to jeopardize safety or to put the organization at risk. Your risk tolerance for those kinds of failures should be very low.

The Coaching Postulate

STAR Leaders™ are coaches that provide mentoring, support, and encouragement while empowering and enabling team members to excel. This leadership extends in all directions and is not just a top-down hierarchy.

E³ Coaching

Encourage

Empower

Enable

Coaches encourage each individual member of their team. They help them learn from mistakes, and they celebrate their successes and achievements.

Coaches empower their teams to excel. Empowerment involves the delegation of authority and the team members' right to make their own decisions.

Coaches enable success. They work behind the scenes to ensure that the team has the necessary resources for success. This includes building the team with the right mix of talent and skill, developing the team with appropriate training, and equipping the team with the necessary tools.

Application of Postulates

You will see these postulates woven throughout the concepts and practical applications discussed in the remainder of this book—beginning with Core Leadership Ideology (CLI) discussed in the following section—and in each component of Tactical and Performance Leadership segments, which are addressed in the second and third books in the *STAR Leadership™ Trilogy*.

What do these postulates mean and why are they important? Simply put, these postulates provide a way to clarify and understand your own world view on leadership. We all have a world view, whether we realize it or not. You can be intentional about shaping it, or you can let it form at whim. If you are intentional about it, you can adjust it, plan it, adapt it, and use it. But being intentional about it requires study, planning, and forethought.

For instance, to apply the foundation postulate, you need to know and understand your purpose in life and the purpose of the organization you serve. If the organization is yours, then you define the purpose. If the organizational purpose is defined by others, make sure you understand it and can align with it.

When your view of leadership aligns with the postulates of the Core Leadership Theory of STAR Leadership™, you understand that leadership is a function of behavior. You can then begin to proactively work on developing and improving your behavior to become the leader that you want to be.

Postulates of STAR Leadership

The Core Leadership Theory of STAR Leadership is built on these seven postulates:

Foundation
Purpose, Principles, Passion, Persistence

Service
Called to serve; Serve to lead & lead to serve

Focus
Results & Relationships

Function
Leadership = f(Behavior)

Alignment
Align purpose & vision

Adaptability
Experience, expertise, priorities, risk tolerance

E^3 Coaching
Encourage, Empower, Enable

As you do this, you will seek to develop and improve behaviors that focus on both results and relationships, and thus become better equipped to set an example as a leader with a solid team that drives positive results.

To further illustrate, let's use a math metaphor. If leadership is a function of behavior, we can integrate that function with respect to incremental improvements in skill (ds), across limits from results to relationships:

$$Leadership = \int_{Results}^{Relationship} \tilde{V} f(Behavior) ds$$

To successfully complete this integration, our behavior must serve a core purpose, and the people that share in that purpose. Our actions, or behaviors, must demonstrate our calling. We should lead so that we may serve and then serve in such a way as to lead others to serve as well. Our behaviors must also communicate a passion for a powerful vision vector™ $(\tilde{V})$ that is properly aligned with this core purpose.[*] These behaviors must coach those that we lead by encouraging, empowering, and enabling success. And the methods we use to coach will need to vary depending on the status of experience, expertise, and priorities evident in any given situation.

We'll discuss more about how to apply these concepts in *Tactical Leadership*.

---

[*] A Vision Vector™ is the combination of Mission and Objectives, as described in the book *STAR Performance*, and is described in greater detail in the section on *Passion* later on in this book.

Core Leadership Ideology

In its essence, Core Leadership Ideology (CLI) is comprised of a worthy cause, rock-solid values, inspiring vision, and consistent devotion. The *worthy cause* is your core *purpose*—it is why you are doing what you are doing. And, while your *principles* define your *rock solid values*, your *passion*, or *inspiring vision*, is built upon your picture of the future—a mission worth accomplishing—and the objectives that will get your mission accomplished. These are the *Three Ps of Strategy*.[53] Lastly, is *consistent devotion*, or *perseverance*, one of the Three Ps of Action (Thompson 49-52).[54] It is foundationally important to STAR Leadership™ because without perseverance leadership will fall.

Long-term success is like running a marathon rather than a sprint. Running with powerful, quick strides is not as important to a marathon runner as it is to a sprinter. Marathon runners must have superior endurance. They must have the tenacity to reach the finish line. The same is true for leaders.

It is the leader's responsibility to define the *Four Ps of STAR Leadership Ideology*— Purpose, Principles, Passion, and Persistence— clearly and concisely communicate them. How you define them, as well as how often you communicate them, determines how you will lead and who will want to follow.

Purpose

Purpose is the most basic, fundamental reason for existing. It is the meaning of life.

The Core Leadership Ideology of STAR Leadership

Purpose
A worthy cause

Principles
Rock solid values

Passion
An inspiring vision

Perseverance
Consistent devotion

Whether we're talking about the life of an individual, a team, a corporation, a non-profit organization, or any other entity, every life has meaning or purpose. For a purpose to drive an organization, the people have to know, understand, and adopt that purpose.

Organizations that are not driven by purpose or meaning are like dust in the wind. They will be carried along by the whims of nature but won't get to their intended destination—at least not with any reasonable efficiency.

It is important to note that this purpose is related to, but distinctly different than, mission. The two terms are often used interchangeably; however, this is a mistake. Purpose answers the questions "why", while mission answers the question "what". Purpose provides meaning while mission provides direction. Purpose is fundamental and unchanging. If you change the purpose, you fundamentally change the nature of the organization. Mission, on the other hand, is fluid and may change over time. Your mission is what you are doing to live out your purpose. If you complete a mission, or find it isn't effectively addressing your purpose, you may need to tweak your mission or change it altogether. As a result, changes to mission over time may be subtle, or they may be intense. Yet, through all the changes to mission, the core purpose remains constant.[55]

As a leader, it is your responsibility to be in touch with your core purpose, to know the meaning of your existence (the existence of your organization). To do this, keep asking yourself "why". "Why is this important?" "Why is this organization valuable to society?"

It isn't enough to know this core purpose for yourself. It is essential that you communicate it continually. It should be written on the walls, talked about at the water cooler, and reviewed in every planning meeting, design review, or project debate. "How does this program or strategic plan fulfill our core purpose?" "How will this design change better accommodate our purpose?" "How does this approach to the project better serve our core purpose?"

Purpose
Your meaning & reason for existing

Principles

There are two aspects of principles should be considered. The first is defining the set of values with which you, as a leader, will live and by which you expect everyone in the organization to abide. The second is a set of pillars that support the "office" of leader.

Like your purpose, you core principles should be constant and unchanging. Over time your adherence to them should improve, but the principles themselves must be fixed forever.

Values

Values, or principles, remain static because once you alter them, they cease to be values. You can't change them to adapt to situations. This is because a core value is something you live by, and something for which you are willing to die. This doesn't mean you can't amend the values to offer clarification over time. Your organization may face situations and circumstances that you may never have imagined, and sometimes these situations will result in confusion about how to interpret and apply the values. Offer clarifications without making fundamental changes to the values themselves.

To clarify this point, consider the Constitution of the United States of America, ratified by our founding fathers in 1787. This document defines the purpose and principles of the United States of America. The opening paragraph, known as the "Preamble to the Constitution," defines the purpose to "form a more perfect Union, establish justice, insure domestic tranquility, provide for the common defense, promote the general welfare, and secure the blessing of liberty to ourselves and our posterity."[56] The seven articles of the Constitution define the principles of this great nation, and the entire document is non-negotiable. Many staked their livelihood, and the lives, to establish it, and since its inception, many more have sacrificed their lives to protect its integrity. Changes to this document are not just semantics; they are a redefinition of the very core of what it means to be the United States of America.

Some contend that the Constitution is a "living document" that does not have a fixed meaning. However, this is a preposterous idea that renders the document meaningless and trivial. The Constitution declares the fundamental purpose and principles of the United States of America. If this purpose and these principles change with the whims of society, then we no longer have a clear definition of what the United States of America actually is. Our founding fathers realized this, and yet they also realized that in the future situations might arise that they couldn't possibly foresee.

For this reason, the Constitution is steadfastly fixed within the preamble "...to form a more perfect Union, establish justice, insure domestic tranquility, provide for the common defense, promote the general welfare, and secure the blessing of liberty to ourselves and our posterity". The principles that define how the US will exist—as described by the Articles of the Constitution—were solidified. Yet the Founding Fathers also provided a means to clarify or adjust them so that they remained pertinent and viable throughout the ages.

The Fifth Article of the Constitution specifically describes how changes, known as amendments, may be made. Just proposing such an amendment requires the approval of a two-thirds majority of either both houses of Congress, or the legislatures of two-thirds of the States. But that doesn't put the changes into effect. It merely allows the changes to be considered. Congress must establish either approval by three-fourths of the State legislatures, or by Conventions in three-fourths of States as the mode of ratification for the amendment.[57] This allows for the possibility of clarification but makes the process of doing so burdensome on purpose, in order to limit the prospects of whimsical changes that could redefine the existence of the United States of America.

However, in the case of the Constitution, we also have historical evidence of such clarifications being made from its beginning. The first amendments were made two years after the Constitution was originally ratified. In 1789, the first set of amendments to the Constitution, known as the Bill of Rights, were ratified. The preamble to the Bill of Rights makes it clear that these amendments do not fundamentally change anything, but rather are intended to clarify and prevent abuse. "The Conventions of a number of the States, having at the time of their adopting the Constitution, expressed a desire, in order to prevent misconstruction or abuse of its powers, that further declaratory and restrictive clauses should be added...."[58]

Principles
Non-negotiable tenants of operation

Your purpose and principles should be just as firm and unchanging as the Constitution of the United States. Just as those who serve as leaders in the government, you and every leader in your organization (which should include every team member) should take an oath to preserve and protect the purpose and principles that define who you are as an organization. It really is that important to your long-term success!

You and every leader in your organization (which should include every team member) should take an oath to preserve and protect the purpose and principles that define who you are as an organization.

It really is that important to your long-term success!

The Seven Pillars of STAR Leadership

In addition to the nonnegotiable principles by which you are striving to live—and for which you are willing to die[†]—there are seven characteristics that I believe are critical elements for leadership to thrive. I call these the *Seven Pillars of STAR Leadership.* These essential elements of leadership are character, courage, confidence, communication, culture, competence, and coaching.

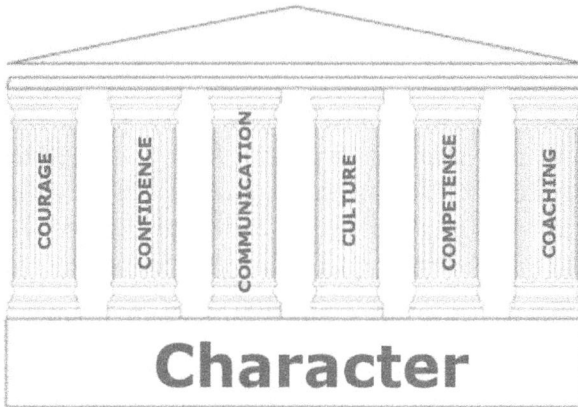

Figure 5. The Seven Pillars of STAR Leadership

[†] Being *non-negotiable* means that you will not give up on these principles – no matter what. *Willing to die* for them may be proverbial, in the sense that you are willing to forego a sale, give up a deal, end a job, or similar. In life-or-death situations, it may also mean a literal willingness to place the ideal, or principle, at a higher level than your own life. What are you willing to die for? What are you willing to take a stand for, no matter the cost? There's a folk proverb that states, "If you don't stand for something, you'll fall for anything." Your principles are what you take a stand for, regardless of what it costs you to do so.

Character is the single most important element of leadership, and it is the foundational cornerstone of STAR Leadership™. Your character determines whom you will lead, and where you will lead them. Will you lead a group of hoodlums and bandits in riots, robberies, and vandalizing? Or will you lead honorable, dedicated people working for a worthy cause? The choice is yours, and it begins and ends with your character.

Character is built upon the smallest decisions that you make every day. Honesty and integrity are not just something you turn on in front of an audience. They are forged by actions taken when no one is looking. For example, character is built by what you do when the cashier at the store gives you an extra quarter in change. Honor isn't activated on the battlefield. It's forged onto the foundation of everyday living—and that honor (or lack thereof) is what shines through in the midst of the battle. The guy that jumps on the grenade to save his team has already spent a lifetime holding doors open for ladies, helping old men cross the street, and giving of himself to help those in need. He doesn't do these actions because people can't get along without him. He does them because they are the polite and honorable thing to do.

Remember the fictional Steve Rogers who desperately tried to join the Army during WWII and ultimately wound up being the scrawny kid on a platform of brutes under review for selection to receive "the serum"? A grenade was tossed into the group of men to see who would react with honor. Every one of them,

> Honor isn't activated on the battlefield. It's forged on the foundation of everyday living.

60

except the scrawny kid from Brooklyn, ran for cover without thinking of anyone else. Little Steve dove on the grenade and screamed for everyone to stay back. It turned out that the grenade was a dummy. He passed the test and became Captain America. But before getting to that "battlefield test", Steve had been a gentleman who treated people with respect and dignity, and he wasn't afraid to stand up for what was right, even if it meant getting beat up in the process.[59]

Your character is determined by the everyday decisions you make. Leaders are people whose character is defined by honor, integrity, reliability, resilience, loyalty, and self-sacrifice.

When we think of a person with "integrity" we think of someone who is honest, trustworthy, and has strong moral principles. This is very true, but integrity is more than this. It is also an ability to hold things together and to bring people together. Consider references to the "hull integrity of a ship," or "the structural integrity of a bridge." Think Titanic or Tacoma Narrows Bridge and their epic integrity failures. The Titanic was *the* unsinkable ship, but she sunk on her maiden voyage. The collapse of the Tacoma Narrows Bridge is a key example for first-year engineering students, signifying the importance of design integrity.

Integrity also represents a consistency of character and a lack of corruption. A person of integrity has character that isn't just skin deep. You know exactly what you're getting each and every time you interact with a person of integrity. You don't have to be afraid to turn your back to a person with integrity.

Integrity

Honest,
trustworthy,
strong moral
principles

Peacemaker
that unifies
people toward
common
objectives

Consistency of
character and
lacks of
corruption

Someone with integrity is respectable because they are honest and trustworthy, because they are peacemakers that strive to unify people toward common objectives, and because they are consistent and dependable in the way that they do things. Integrity also feeds reliability because reliability is about being dependable and about consistency of results. When people of good character tell you that they will get something done, you can rely on them doing everything humanly possible because of the consistency of their character. Because they are consistent, you know they will be reliable.

Resilience is the ability to adapt when faced with adversity. Strong character demands excessive adaptability because adversity is guaranteed in almost every pursuit worth investing time. The resilient not only adapt and survive, but they also adapt and overcome. Strong character is resilient in the face of trauma. It enables people to bounce back from hard times, stressful situations, and seemingly overwhelming challenges. When we face such challenges, we have a choice. We can respond with fear, anxiety, worry, and depression, or we can respond with urgency, attentiveness, and thoughtful action.

Even though STAR Leaders™ are loyal, it doesn't mean they never fire anyone. Sometimes firing poor performers is required to remain loyal to the organization or to the cause. And, it is likely to be in the best interest of the poor performer as well.

Loyalty is about fidelity, allegiance, or devotion to a cause or a team. It is steadfast faithfulness even in the face of hardship or temptation. Leaders with poor character are loyal only to themselves, and they will stab you in the back if it provides their desired outcome.

Leaders of sound character will hold their team members accountable, and they will also stand up for them. They offer praise in public and will correct team members privately. I've had leaders publicly scold me, as if they believed humiliation is the best motivator. Even if what they said were true, they didn't earn my respect. On the other hand, I've also had leaders privately correct me in a gentle and loyal manner. These leaders won my respect every time, whether or not they were in the right.

To develop a strong character, you simply have to make the right choices: The choice to be honest and exhibit true integrity, and the choice to put in the required effort to be reliable and resilient. These choices require self-sacrifice. Leaders that put themselves first will cut corners, take short-cuts, and run over others to get what they want. Leaders who exhibit self-sacrifice will put the needs of others ahead of themselves. This sacrificial approach is what it takes to be a servant leader and to possess the character of a STAR Leader™.

Character
Integrity
Reliability
Resilience
Loyalty

Courage

Accomplishing something meaningful is challenging because the path to success is filled with obstacles and failures. Reaching the destination will take courage. Courage isn't the absence of fear. It is bravery that results in action in the face of fear.

Leadership requires courage. It takes courage to be the first to face a challenge. It takes courage to persevere when the obstacles seem overwhelming. It takes courage to get back up and try again when failure knocks you down. Success requires action, and action requires courage.

Courage isn't an absence of fear; rather, it is the boldness to proceed in the face of fear.

If character is the cornerstone, courage is the primary buttress holding leadership in place. A buttress is a structural component that is built to support a wall or post, and courage structurally supports leadership. Leadership must endure obstacles and challenges. It takes courage to face them, and even more to lead a team into the face of adversity.

Courage is synonymous with bravery. It isn't an absence of fear; rather, it is the boldness to proceed in the face of fear. Leadership is influence, and it is about creating change. No worthwhile change has ever occurred without resistance. A leader will face internal resistance to change, adversity for the change effort itself, and external resistance pushing against the direction being pursued. The kind of daring boldness required to keep pressing on despite adversity and resistance is bravery. This is central to what it means to have courage.

Courage is more than just being brave in the face of fear. It is a demonstration of determination. It is a decisive mobility that is resolute on what is most important—standing firm on purpose while demonstrating agility in methods. This kind of steadfast commitment is an essential component of courage.

Bravery and determination are fed by fortitude. This is a mental strength that doesn't back down from a challenge. Fortitude is not stubbornness. It isn't about locking onto something and never seeing the alternatives. It's about the strength of character to face difficulty, adversity, or danger. It's mental toughness. It is a resilient character that requires courage to persevere in the face of adversity.

Our "spirit" is what gives us fortitude and determination. Spirit is the animation of courage. The Okinawan culture, and the martial art of karate, refers to the *tanden* of a person, which is the outward expression of the internal desire to win or succeed. A literal translation of the word *tanden* is belly, abdomen, or gut. However, the conceptual translation is more meaningful. It describes the source of energy, will, desire, and the internal motivating force of a person that allows him or her to persevere through any type of adversity. Karate practitioners train to drive their movements from the *tanden*, that is, to center their every motion from the gut—both in the physical sense of "leading with the belly" and in the emotional sense of "leading with a warrior spirit".[60]

This boldness is a spirit of tenacity that can't be stopped. It is an essential element of courage. Without it, mustering the courage to carry on when the challenge is overwhelming will be nearly impossible. Yet, with this boldness and tenacity, one's courage is empowered and unstoppable.

Courage leads directly back to the cornerstone of leadership, which is character. It takes a strong and self-sacrificing character to demonstrate heroic courage that puts the needs of others (the needs of the team) ahead of oneself. Whether this selfless courage is demonstrated on an actual battlefield, or in the day-to-day operations of a business, valor requires strong character.

Some people are just born with a courageous spirit. They leap into action when action is needed most. Truthfully, most of us need to cultivate this spirit. Doing so requires prioritizing the cultivation of character in daily actions. Bravery that isn't tempered by character isn't valor. At best it's just thrill-seeking, and, more often, it is closer to stupidity.

You have probably seen the guy who fancies himself brave because he's always up for a challenge. He will try almost any stunt on a dare and will recklessly put himself into danger just for the thrill of it. Now, I'm not condemning intense roller coaster rides, extreme sports, rock climbing, or bungie jumping. These are all legitimate ways to seek a thrill and can challenge us to face fears. However, participating in thrill-seeking activities does not make one courageous. Courage is not about seeking danger. Instead, it's about responding with bravery, determination, fortitude, spirit, and valor when danger and adversity find you. Courage enables you to do the right thing or make progress toward a greater vision.

As you cultivate your character and become passionate about your vision, be courageous in facing adversity that is sure to come your way.

Courage
Bravery
Determination
Fortitude
Tenacious Spirit
Valor

Confidence

Confidence is about having a knack for sound judgment and discernment. It's about getting results. There is an enormous difference between confidence and arrogance. Confidence is being filled with trust, certainty and self-assurance. It results from a foundation of character and courage. Arrogance stems from being filled with conceit, pride, and a sense of self-importance.

Confident leaders trust in their team and inspire action because they believe in themselves and their colleagues. No one wants to follow an arrogant individual who thinks he or she is better than others. However, one who exhibits a quiet calmness, along with a sense of urgency in the face of a challenge, is a leader

Confidence is about having good discernment, sound judgement, and a passionate desire to see the team succeed.

around which people will rally. Colin Powell says, when you face a challenge, "assess the situation, move fast, be decisive, but remain calm and never let them see you sweat."[61] That's confidence!

Confidence isn't about always being right either. No one is always right. Confidence is about having good discernment, sound judgement, and a passionate desire to see the team succeed. It's the leader's responsibility to make the final decisions, but only a foolish leader doesn't seek the counsel of the team whenever possible. Many times, I've been certain that I knew what to do in a particular situation but still talked to several team members and trusted advisors before acting. Often the result is a tweak in my plan, and sometimes it is a complete reversal of direction that saved me a lot of grief.

Confidence is the pulse, or heartbeat, of leadership. A healthy pulse varies in frequency as it reacts during rest, exercise, or adrenalin surges, and no pulse at all means life has been lost. Similarly, without confidence, one cannot lead. Without proper preparation and *exercise* our confidence is weak, like the pulse of a couch potato. This results in weak action, or total inaction, and isn't a quality of good leadership. At the opposite extreme, overconfidence is like the adrenaline junky that continues to leap into harm's way just for the thrill, or over reacts to a challenge in order to make a scene. That kind of behavior will eventually catch up with you.

The mastery of true confidence is only possible with intentional practice, learning from mistakes, knowing your limits, and building a coalition of trustworthy people upon which you can lean. A well-disciplined and well-practiced athlete has a powerful and effective heartbeat. Similarly, a well-disciplined and well-practiced leader has the strength of confidence.

Care must be taken to not be over-confident. Overconfidence results from pride. Having an arrogant sense of always being right will destroy a leader, and the organization that he or she serves. Perhaps you have heard the proverb, "Pride goes before destruction, and a haughty spirit before a fall."[62]

Arrogance will lead us to make rash judgments, irrational plans, and poor investments, which destroy teams.   On the surface, arrogance may seem like confidence. Yet, confidence builds and sustains the remaining pillars of leadership, while arrogance ultimately tears them down.

Arrogance is inwardly focused and based upon "I". Confidence is outwardly focused and built on "us." The "I" mentality will always lead to destruction in the long run because organizational success cannot be sustained over time without good leadership that builds and promotes confidence across the team.

Confidence is an assurance that you and your team have the talent, focus, and ability necessary to achieve the task at hand—or that you can acquire missing talent and ability through training or team building.   This assurance is built on making certain that things get done. It is a removal of doubt within yourself and your team that the task can be accomplished. It is taking the steps necessary to assure everyone involved that "We can do this!"

Confidence is also about reliability. An arrogant response to challenges always responds with a resounding "yes". A confident response will recognize the weaknesses and risks, communicate them effectively to all stakeholders, and bring the team together to identify what is needed to achieve success. A confident leader doesn't make blind promises that can't be fulfilled. Instead, a confident leader sets a high and realistic standard while being completely honest and open about the risks involved and the resources that will be needed.

A confident leader is both reliable and dependable. These two qualities are closely related, and some might say they are really the same thing. The reason that I categorize them separately is because reliability refers to skills, while dependability refers to heart or spirit. A confident leader has both reliable skills and a dependable spirit. He or she won't give up until the job is done and done right.

A confident leader is both reliable and dependable.

This is why the foundation of the character cornerstone is so important. A great leader exudes confidence that is trustworthy. This doesn't mean that the leader never makes mistakes. Quite the contrary, mistakes are a part of taking risks, and taking risks are what a leader does. What it does mean is that great leaders are honest with both stakeholders and their teams about the risks and potential rewards of any initiative.

Furthermore, a great leader won't intentionally mislead the team or the stakeholders. When leaders with character make mistakes, they take ownership. There is no blame shifting, nor is there any sweeping it under the proverbial rug. Great leaders recognize their mistakes, learn from them, and strive to avoid the same mistake in the future. They are honest with themselves about how the mistake took place, and they are honest with the team and stakeholders about what it will take to get past the mistake. They will strive to turn all mistakes into successes. They know that the challenges in the process are real but not insurmountable. Their confidence in themselves and in their team is well placed as they move to face these challenges.

There are two kinds of confidence, and both require intentional behavior because confidence doesn't happen by accident. The first is self-confidence, and the second is team confidence.

Self-confidence is built on experience. Leaders must step out and make decisions—Including bad ones—in order to learn the life lessons required to build confidence. Self-confidence built on anything less than experience is approaching arrogance. Avoid the temptation to become arrogant as strongly as you guard yourself from the temptation to lack confidence.

Be confident that you desire to succeed. Be confident that sometimes you will fail. Be confident that failure is acceptable, as long as you learn from it. Have the courage to continue, and, most importantly, make sure that your confidence is built upon good character.

Great leaders must be confident in themselves. Even more importantly, great leaders must have confidence in those around them. Just as self-confidence doesn't rule out the possibility of the leader making a mistake, team confidence doesn't rule out the possibility of the team, or individuals on the team, making mistakes. In fact, this should be encouraged. Not that we want our teams to make careless mistakes, but we do need our teams to be pushing their limits and taking risks. Doing this will most certainly result in mistakes, and a great leader guides the team to learn from them rather than to be demoralized by them.

To further illustrate, let's make an analogy to 'home runs'. If I asked how often you hit a 'home run' in your efforts to achieve your goals, would you answer maybe 70%? Maybe you're just 50/50? Maybe you only hit the 'home run' 10% of the time, and think poorly of yourself as a result? Well, consider the top three home run hitters in baseball history: Barry Bonds, Hank Aaron, and Babe Ruth. These guys are the home run kings. No one would question this. Would you believe that the home run kings had career records for percentage of at-bats resulting in a homerun of 7.7%, 6.1%, and 8.5% respectively?[63] The greatest of these percentages belongs to the legendary Babe Ruth, yet he only hit a home run 8.5% of the time that he went up to bat. Your 10% doesn't look so bad now, does it?

This doesn't mean that every other at bat resulted in an out. Some of them did, and others got them on base without getting home runs. The same will be true for you and your team. Sometimes your efforts will get you close to the target (base hit), and sometimes you'll miss the mark completely (strike out). Learn from every "at-bat" experience, and you will begin to put fear in the hearts of your competitors because there will be a 6-9% chance you'll hit a home run any time you step up to the plate.

By the way, Babe Ruth wasn't afraid to take risks and swing for the fences. This resulted in his 8.5% home run stat, and it also meant he struck out 15.8% of the time.[64] He was nearly two times more likely to strike out, than he was to hit a home run, yet the competition was always afraid of that home run potential.

So cultivating confidence begins with cultivating character in yourself and in your teams. Have the courage to take risks and learn from them when failures occur. Coach those that you lead to embrace the risks and work together with confidence and passion toward common goals.

Confidence
Judgment
Discernment
Trust
Decisive
Calm & Collected
Experienced

Communication

Communication is the key to success in any team endeavor. If your team isn't communicating, how does it know what to do or when to do it? Leaders must communicate what they know with the team, they must draw out the information they need from the team, and they must ensure that team members are openly and freely communicating with each other.

A leader develops a vision and communicates that vision clearly and confidently. Communication is more about listening than talking. It's about asking the right questions and listening for the important answers. You can't be a good communicator if you're not a good listener.

Communication is a two-way street. Leaders take responsibility, and to do so, leaders must have the information needed to be responsible. Colin Powell said, "Leaders need to know ground truth and not just what they get from reports and staff."[65] You can't hide in an ivory tower if you're going to lead. Having influence requires having and sharing information that is important and relevant.

Communication is the infrastructure of leadership because it is the fundamental means by which ideas are shared, instructions are provided, and vision is clarified. When the communication pathways are not open, it is difficult, if not impossible, to get things done. When we aren't communicating, or aren't communicating effectively, then we aren't working together as a team to our fullest potential.

On the battlefield, military leaders know that it is essential to maintain open paths for communications, supplies, and troop movements. Communications is the first target of attack, because if your enemies can't communicate among themselves, they can't coordinate their response. The same is true in any business or organizational setting. If we are to achieve our maximum potential—working together as a team—we must maintain open lines of communication.

Communication is more than simply a means of exchanging information. Before we can freely and openly share information that is received and acted upon in a trusting and passionate manner, we must lay the foundation of a strong relationship. Think of the bond of "brotherhood" that exists among the top teams. Whether it is Seal Team Six, your favorite sports team, the local police force, or the crew of Fire House No. 7, the bond of relationship is essential to successful completion of the mission.

The key to effective communication is getting to know the people on your team. As a leader, it is essential that you have genuine concern for your team members' well-being—not just the well-being of the mission. John C. Maxwell lists listening as one of "The 21 Indispensable Qualities of a Leader" in his book by that same title. He states that "Good leaders, the kind that people want to follow, do more than conduct business when they interact with followers. They take the time to get a feel for who each one is as a person."[66] I couldn't agree with this more. Getting to know your team members will ultimately make the job of focusing on the mission easier.

> Listening should be the most used tool in our communication tool set.

Listening should be the most used tool in your communication tool set. The good Lord gave us twice as many ears as He did a mouth. We should all remember this before we speak by making sure that we listen at least twice as much as we talk. Thousands of years ago, this wisdom was proclaimed in an ancient Hebrew proverb that states, "Even a fool who keeps silent is considered wise; when he closes his lips, he is deemed intelligent."[67]

We need to listen for facts and information, but we also need to listen for tones, emotions, body language and other forms of communications. Dale Carnegie states, "If you aspire to be a good conversationalist, be an attentive listener."[68] Listening is the key to opening doors. It allows you to build relationships, and it enables you to gain more information than speaking does.

In addition to listening, the Socratic Questioning method, a powerful tool, can help you gain a deeper understanding of other people's perspectives, thought processes, and character.[69] This art of questioning can also help others understand your perspectives, too.

For example, we not only need to understand what others think, but we also want to invite the persons with whom we converse to explore their own thought processes. Asking questions, such as "Why do you say that?" or "Could you provide further explanation?", encourages them to provide more insight by thinking more introspectively and critically as well.

Questions can also be used to challenge assumptions by asking "Is this always the case?" or "Why do you make that assumption?" To better understand the basis for an argument, questions, such as "Why do you say that?" or "How do you know that is true?" can help illuminate the differences between truth and unjustified responses.

Questions can be used to encourage alternative perspectives. When we ask questions, such as "Is there any other approach we should consider?" or "Are there any alternative ways of considering this data?", we encourage positive thought and consideration. A line of questioning like this also helps introduce our own thoughts or perspectives in a positive manner, which makes those listening to us more receptive. Questions such as these promote better discussion and consideration. And, through questioning, we may even find that our original perspective was not the best approach.

Questions can also be used to enhance discussions on the consequences and implications of a particular course of action when we ask leading questions, such as "But if this happened, what else would result?" Finally, we can respond to questions with questions. We may be responding to what we've been asked with a question like "Which of your questions turned out to be most useful?" We may also further our own questions by asking, "Why do you think I asked that question?" or "Why do you think my question was important?"

Another use of communication, perhaps one of the most important applications of communication, is to praise members of your team, when praise is due. STAR Leaders™ understand the importance of showing appreciation for those with whom they work. Dale Carnegie defines this as Principle No. 6, in the nine principles of being a leader. He states, "Praise the slightest improvement and praise every improvement. Be hearty in your approbation and lavish in your praise."[70] To be honest, I believe that such recognition of effort and achievement is the single best means of inspiring anyone to be passionate about performance. The reverse of this is true as well.

If accomplishment and achievement is simply expected, and never acknowledged, the lack of acknowledgement will take the wind out of anyone's sails.

On the other hand, leaders may also need to go to their communications tool box to provide critical feedback. While criticism is never an easy pill to swallow, it is crucial that we avoid hiding problems or letting bad behavior go unchecked. When we need to deliver bad news or critique poor performance, it is best to do so swiftly and quietly. Wielding a proverbial hammer in our conversation is useless. It may correct the problem in the short term, but it will certainly create animosity and distrust. Correction and reproof should be delivered in a positive tone. In our delivery, we should note mistakes of our own, highlight good effort and positive results that the recipient of the critique has made, and then deliver the critique in a caring yet firm tone with the positive message of learning from the mistake.

Still, some leaders will tell you that people just don't listen unless you speak harshly and assertively. However, those who believe so have weak leadership skills because they lack the experience and discipline to handle such situations in a positive manner. Those that they lead likely lack respect for them, and only follow because of the positional authority granted to the leader.

Don't misunderstand. There may be times when harsh words and difficult actions are required. My point is simply that if an individual requires harsh words to respond positively on a regular basis, he or she is likely not someone you really want on your team anyway. Being a great leader requires the self-disciple to respond to failures in a manner that improves the team and the individual, rather than humiliating anyone.

Debating, too, is a crucial part of communication. It is the best way to address multiple alternatives and hash out the pros and cons of each. A good debate involves sharing ideas and information freely without fear of being attacked. A STAR Leader™ encourages debate and carefully guides the debate process to ensure that all ideas and perspectives are given the courtesy and respect of consideration, and that these ideas are discussed openly and freely in a manner that guides the team to the best possible solution.

Lastly, the most obvious reason for communication is the sharing of information. This, of course, is one of the purposes of communication, and that is why it is so important to keep the lines of communication flowing freely.

As part of this information exchange, it is critical that bad news be received as openly as good news. Bad news and problems don't go away just because we don't talk about them. For a leader, it is imperative that problems be voiced so that they can be addressed. When those that you lead believe that the bearer of bad news will be attacked and martyred, they are not likely to bring this information to your attention. But when your team knows that you are less interested in placing blame than in finding solutions and learning how to avoid the problem in the future, they will feel free to share good as well as bad news.

Therefore, our ability to communicate with those that we lead is essential to the success of our teams and our organizations. Without clear, open lines of communication, there really isn't any leadership. To be great leaders, we must communicate continually with those that we lead.

Communication
Listen
Question
Lavish Praise
Gentle Critique
Open Debate
Clarify Vision
Share Information
Provide Instruction
Enable Coordination
Build Relationships

Culture

A STAR Leader™ cultivates culture. Like character, culture is cultivated with day-to-day decisions and actions. Culture is cultivated by setting an example and demonstrating that culture.

A STAR Leader™ cultivates a culture of loyalty, duty, service and vision. Loyalty is caring about the people you lead as much as the mission on which you are leading them. The mission comes first, but the people are integral to how that mission is accomplished. If you want to lead, you must first develop a culture of loyalty. Dale Carnegie said, "You can make more friends in two months by becoming genuinely interested in other people than in two years by trying to get other people interested in you."[71]

Duty is about fulfilling one's obligations. In a culture of duty, there is a keen sense of accountability among peers. While team members realize that their leader will hold them accountable, they also—more importantly—do not want to let their teammates down. They will thus strive to fulfill their obligations and communicate problems to both the team and to leadership when they are having difficulty meeting expectations. By setting the example and demonstrating a strong worth ethic, leaders can develop this culture of duty. They should not expect their team members to have a stronger work ethic than themselves.

A culture of service is one in which every member of the team acts as a unit and serves one another. It requires self-sacrifice and dedication. Leaders are servants first—not in the sense that they become subservient, but in the sense that they actively serve the interest of their team above their own. A servant leader will inspire the same in others, thus developing a culture of service that results in an unstoppable team.

Furthermore, a team with vision is a team that is on fire. It is a team filled with passion for a cause in which each team member firmly believes. It is the leader who inspires that cause and, with it, a strong sense of purpose.

Culture is the sustainer of leadership because culture is the set of behavioral norms and common principles (values) within the organization. It's been said that "culture consists of group norms of behavior and the

> Culture is the sustainer of leadership because culture is the set of behavioral norms and common principles (values) within the organization.

underlying shared values that help keep those norms in place."[72] The behavioral norms and shared values are what sustains the efforts of leadership. In fact, these norms and values are also a direct result of the efforts of leadership. Therefore, an organization's culture is both a result of leadership, and it is also a sustainer of leadership.

The culture of an organization acts as a sustainer of leadership when the values of the leader are widely adopted by the organization. This requires great effort on the part of the leader, and this requirement is ongoing. There is an ancient Japanese proverb that states, "Learning through practice is like pushing a cart up a hill: If you slack off, it will slip backward."[73] The same is true for the establishment of values by leadership. If leaders slack off in their communication and adherence to values, the culture will become less important, with team members merely providing lip service.

In addition to values, culture is also heavily influenced by vision and by the story of the organization that provides purpose and passion. "Culture is a carrier of meaning. Culture provides not only a shared view of 'what is' but also of 'why is'. In this view, culture is about 'the story' in which people in the organization are embedded, and the values and rituals that reinforce that narrative."[74]

In a prior book, "STAR Performance," I describe the foundations of strategy as purpose, principle, and passion.[75] This strategic foundation is, in effect, a major contributor to the forming of culture for an organization. When the people of an organization share a common purpose, a common set of principles (values),

82

and a passion for the vision, then the behavioral norms of the organization will be reflected in their culture.

Culture is both created by leadership and sustained by leadership. In a culture of leadership, the expectation is set for all members in the organization to be leaders. The old paradigm that leadership is strictly top-down no longer works effectively. Successful organizations must find ways to grow beyond being led by an org chart. This isn't to say that there is not a leader creating vision, but rather that the organization as a whole is adopting a leadership mentality.

In other words, leaders in the organization know that part of their role as a leader is to cultivate new leaders. They must be mentoring and training a next generation of leaders. I know many readers are going to respond with the old attitude that "leaders are born, not made" or "you can't teach leadership – you've either got it, or you don't." Clearly leadership comes more naturally to some, and others have to work at it. Yet, the skills and abilities required to be a leader are, without a doubt, learnable skills. One might be born with a natural ability to lead, but no one is born with fully developed leadership skills. Almost anyone can develop such skills, at least to some extent. We all need to work at developing these skills, and great leaders recognize the importance of mentoring others in the development of these skills.

One of the world's most renowned experts on organizational change, John Kotter, states that the traditional model of *born leaders* is erroneous. Speaking of this idea, he states, "…the historically dominant concept takes leadership skills as a divine gift of birth, a gift granted to a small number of people." He continues to explain, however, that this concept doesn't match observations he's made in decades of studying organizations. He says, "...the older model is nearly oblivious to the power and the potential of lifelong learning."[76] In other words, the key to a leadership culture, in which leaders are continually being developed, is a culture of lifelong learning.

This type of leadership culture is a force multiplier. Remember that leadership is not about position on an org chart. You can be a leader in any position, at any level, at any pay-grade, in any organization. An organization filled with leaders doesn't mean that everyone is the CEO. It means that the CEO doesn't have to directly address many issues within the organization because the team takes the initiative to find solutions on its own. There isn't a culture of fear in which office politics and cut-throat competition kill teamwork, but rather a culture where individual performance is led by peer accountability and a universal desire to avoid letting the team down.

A culture of leadership is one in which solutions are more important than blame. In this type of culture, team members are not afraid to bring up 'bad news'. Instead, everyone is so focused on improvement and problem solving that when problems do arise, everyone is competing to be the first to help solve them, rather than competing for glory. Jim Collins said that "Leadership is about vision and creating a climate where truth is heard and confronted."[77] (Collins). The culture of leadership insists on hearing the truth—even when it's painful to hear (and, *especially* when it's painful to hear). In cultures that fear the truth, problems that exist beneath the surface often don't get addressed. This either holds inefficiencies in place or kills the organization completely.

In a culture of leadership, vision, mission, and objectives are constantly being communicated. In fact, communications become a way of life rather than messages that need to be heard. Conversations in the hallway revolve around the vision. Breakroom small talk will focus on the vision. You won't even be able to get a cup of coffee without stumbling across talk of the vision in some fashion. It will be so prevalent that it is a part of nearly every conversation and drives nearly every action.

The characteristics of culture in any given organization will reflect the leadership and the vision (or lack thereof) of the organization. A strong culture with great potential will have characteristics reflecting a sense of urgency yet will also maintain a perspective that patience is required to succeed. The members of this type of organization exude a sense of empowerment and trust that results in strong teamwork. The entire organization will be focused on the same objectives. Peer accountability will be the norm, and leaders will provide ample recognition when someone does exemplary work.

The characteristics of culture in any given organization will reflect the leadership and the vision (or lack thereof) of the organization.

The opposite is true for weaker cultures. Complacency will permeate the organization, resulting in little or no ability to make needed changes. Anxiety will overwhelm the team members and silos will replace empowerment, such that things can't get done without going through unnecessary organizational restraints or bottlenecks. Egos and mistrust will limit or destroy teamwork. Attention will be focused on overly bureaucratic processes instead of common objectives. Blame will replace accountability while tyranny is accepted as the norm instead of self-discipline.

While no organization is perfect, the focus should be on developing organizations with a strong and successful culture of winning. To do this, we must develop a culture of leadership within our organizations. We need to be intentional about multiplying leadership through mentoring. We need to be intentional about communicating vision, mission, and objectives. We need to be adamant about our principles and ensure that they are adopted uniformly across the organization. When we do these things, we will find teamwork, loyalty, and success because a culture that cultivates and encourages the same will be the result.

Culture
Behavioral Norms
Common Principles
Sustains Leadership
Carrier of Meaning
Reflects Sense of Purpose and Vision

Competence

Leaders must demonstrate competence. This doesn't mean that they need to have expertise in all areas of the organization. However, they should be proficient in at least one area of interest. Additionally, leaders also know how to draw from the competencies of the team. In other words, one of a leader's greatest competencies is team building.

The leader must have knowledge and capability. Competent leaders will inspire competent people to join them on their mission. Furthermore, a competent leader will not be afraid to delegate to the members of the team.

Competence is the fuel of leadership. While it is the fuel, competence alone doesn't make one a leader, yet without competence, becoming influential in a positive manner is extremely difficult (if not impossible).

Generally speaking, competence is simply the ability to do something, to complete some task, or to perform some function. It refers to possessing the required skills, knowledge, and abilities to perform in a particular role.

Performing in the role of a leader often requires a "jack-of-all-trades" kind of ability. In some cases, it will require specific expertise in a particular field. Regardless of industry, discipline, or organizational type, every leader must possess, and regularly exercise, certain leadership skills, attributes, and behaviors. These include being a good listener, prioritizing a connection with people about what's important to them, building bridges that promote communication and teamwork, keeping the flow of information open, and demonstrating habitual commitment to lifelong learning.

This is not an exhaustive list, but it is a good starting place. Being a great leader requires developing and sustaining great leadership behaviors, skills and habits. Constantly studying what these behaviors are, how they promote leadership ability, and how to effectively exercise them is essential to improving leadership.

Competence in the area of building teams is another essential component of great leadership. No matter how skilled you may be, you can't do it alone. Being a great leader requires building teams that work well together and complement one another. As the leader, you will have certain strengths and certain weaknesses. And, your team should be built upon focusing your time and energy on your strengths and placing others in complementary roles that fill in for your weaknesses.

In addition to the initial building of the team, great leaders know how to set an example of continuous development. They will proactively demonstrate the attribute of lifelong learning and encourage every team member to develop and improve their own skills. Sometimes this will involve team training that teaches the same skills to every time member. At others, it will involve individualized development that provides specific training opportunities for individuals on the team.

Competence is possessing the required skills, knowledge, and abilities to perform in a particular role.

For instance, all team members should receive leadership development training and coaching, general financial management training, and communication skills training. As individuals, team members should receive specific training and development for skills directly related to their specific tasks, such as an advanced programming refresher for code developers, a GAAP refresher for accountants, a seminar in leading trends in circuit layout for electrical engineers, or an updated network infrastructure overview for an IT leader.

Leaders must possess an overarching general management competency that extends across their entire range of responsibility. This does not mean that leaders must be experts with regard to every particular detail within the scope of their responsibility, but it does mean that they must possess a general knowledge and understanding of how things work.

In the C-suite, this means a general knowledge and understanding of the entire organization. The CEO does not need to be an expert accountant, production supervisor, purchasing agent, IT director, product developer, and inventory controller. The CEO does need to understand each of these functions well enough to know when they are operating smoothly and when there is problem. CEOs also need to have enough knowledge in each area to comprehend the information that their team is sharing, and know which questions need to be asked.

The same is true for leaders at every level within the organization. Every leader will have some specific expertise and an ever-increasing general knowledge base from which to lead a team or organization. In fact, the trend in business is to place CEOs with an increasing breadth of experience in multiple areas of discipline. In order of rank, the top seven CEO-producing functions for CEOs of S&P 500 companies are [1] finance, [2] operations and marketing (tied), [4] sales, [5] engineering, [6] planning & development, and [7] law. It's no wonder that it's becoming quite uncommon to find a CEO that has spent an entire career in a single functional discipline. In fact, as of 2004, only 9% of S&P 500 company CEOs hail from single function careers, a drop from 25% over a five-year period.[78] In another study, it was found that 30% of Fortune 500 CEOs possessed a strong financial background from some point in their careers, but that only about 5% came from CFO roles. More than half of the CEOs came from COO or President positions, indicating that an operations background is as important as finance to Fortune 500 companies. In fact, "though they [CEOs] often began their careers in finance, the executives who have made it to the top are those who have successfully used their financial expertise to become excellent operators."[79]

From the CEO statistics noted above, it is apparent that a great leader does not need to be in the CEO position of the org chart. Great leadership can, and should, exist on every rung of the corporate ladder and every level of the org chart. Great leadership is about behavior, not position! Great leadership is behavior that demonstrates character, strong work ethic, reliability, and an eagerness to play an active role in problem-solving. This can be demonstrated from any functional role at any level in an organizational hierarchy.

Be a leader no matter your function. Focus on your strengths and surround yourself with those whose strengths complement your weaknesses. Learn to relate, encourage, and build up those around you. Develop depth in your particular area of expertise and breadth across a range of functions that allows you to understand your organization from a "bigger picture" perspective.

Competence
Proficiency
Team Building
Delegates
Leadership Behaviors

Coaching

Every leader is part coach. A leader will develop a learning environment in which a drive to learn and do new things is deeply ingrained into the culture because duty and service require learning new things.

Like every great coach, a leader doesn't care who gets the credit. In fact, Colin Powell teaches that "When something goes well, make sure you share the credit down and around the whole organization.... When things go badly, it is your fault, not theirs."[80] Of team members, he also said, "They want to be the best they can be; a good leader lets them know it when they are."[81]

More than letting others know when they've done a good job, a leader holds them accountable with positive and constructive criticism. A leader invests time and energy into making others better at what they do. The leader invests time into mentoring others to develop them and the team into being leaders themselves.

Coaches do certain things to help others improve and excel. A coach listens. Listening is probably the single most important thing that a coach must do every day. Learning requires attentive listening. When someone is talking, they are sharing information. This information may be job-related, culture-related, personal in nature, etc. When people listen, they have the opportunity to pick up on subtle clues to deeper truths which they may otherwise have not been aware. Leaders may discover the root of a problem by listening to a team member explain what happened. They may learn of personal challenges that are influencing a team member's productivity and perhaps be able to help. They may let the speaker know that they care, simply because they took the time to listen.

Dale Carnegie lists twelve principles for "how to win people to your way of thinking." Principle number six is "let the other person do a great deal of the talking."[82] He also said, "There are two very good reasons to listen to other people. You learn things that way, and people respond to those who listen to them."[83] John C. Maxwell said, "A good leader encourages followers to tell him what he needs to know, not what he wants to hear."[84]

Everyone needs encouragement. And, a great coach knows how to provide the encouragement that people need. When people are depressed about failure, adversity, competition, fear, or anything else, they need encouragement to lift them up. Sometimes encouragement is a simple "You can do it" or "Don't be afraid." Sometimes it takes the form of a helping hand that assists with getting the task complete and showing that it can be done.

An example of this is found in the Bible. When Jesus came to His disciples walking on water, they did not recognize Him at first and trembled with fear. Sensing their fear, Jesus spoke out to them saying, "Take heart; It is I. Do

Everyone needs encouragement. A great coach knows how to provide the encouragement that people need when they are down and out.

not be afraid."[85]   He knew their need for encouragement and provided reassurance. When one of His disciples, Peter, asked permission to join Him, Jesus simply replied, "Come," and "Peter got out of the boat and walked on the water and came to Jesus."[86] Shortly thereafter, Peter realized what he was doing and quickly became afraid and started sinking. In panic he cried out to Jesus, "Lord, save me." Before anything else, "Jesus immediately reached out his hand and took hold of him,"[87] thus providing the encouragement in the form of immediate assistance that Peter so desperately needed. Here, we see the greatest leader of all time provide a spectacular example of leadership by demonstrating encouragement with words and action.

A great coach also knows how to celebrate wins with the team. If wins are not celebrated, people will assume that their efforts haven't been appreciated and won't perform at their best.

At times, a coach must also provide reproof. In the example discussed above where Jesus provides encouragement to His disciples, He also provides reproof. After helping Peter back into the boat, He said, "O you of little faith, why did you doubt?"[88] There is no indication that this was said with anger or malice. Instead, it appears that Jesus spoke to Peter with a soft, corrective, yet reassuring voice, to let him know that he could have done it had he simply had faith.

We need to realize that people on our teams will make mistakes, and that we need to let them. Don't ignore the mistakes, however, point them out in a gentle and productive tone that helps your team members learn rather than feel disheartened. To illustrate, consider this example. Early in my career, I generated a report for a project I'd been working on and circulated it for proofreading to a few people who had helped on the project. From their critique, I learned that I had made a few typos in the report. Some mistakes were made that would have caused great confusion had it been widely circulated. Because of this, my manager called me into a "private conference" and proceeded to blast me with a sizeable amount of anger and attitude.

For what seemed like an eternity, I listened to him belittle me, tell me how stupid I was, insist that my education had been fruitless, and describe how he didn't like having me on his team. That reproof was deserved. I did make the mistakes. But the way in which the reproof was delivered was foolish and ineffective. I began looking for a new employer that afternoon, but before I could make a change for myself, he made a sudden move of his own and left the company. I always wondered if he left on his own, or if someone a rung or two higher up the corporate ladder saw his behavior and decided they didn't want him on their team?

My point is simple. Give reproof in a positive, corrective, and supportive manner. Everyone makes mistakes, and people will learn from them if you help them do so. When you belittle them or come down on them with a forceful vengeance, you don't promote learning, you only promote anger and defensive behavior. John Wooden said, "A coach is someone who can give correction without causing resentment."[89]

Great coaches know how to ask the right questions. In fact, asking questions and listening to the responses is likely the most important aspect to coaching. Asking questions does three key things for you and your team: [1] It provides you and your team with important information, [2] it awakens thought on issues and opportunities, and [3] it encourages dialogue across the team that may uncover more efficient solutions and new ideas.

When you ask questions, you drive people to think. Sometimes they'll know the answer right away, and other times it will stir up thought processes that make them think about the situation differently. Earlier, I presented the use of a technique called "Socratic Questioning" (named for the Greek philosopher and teacher, Socrates, ca. 470-399 BC) in the section on communication. It is such an important and valuable technique that it is worth reviewing again.

This technique involves asking questions as if you know nothing about the topic (whether this is true or not) in order to cause the people being asked to think through the topic, dig deeper into their knowledge base, and develop their ability to think critically.[90] There are six basic types of questions to use in this manner:[91]

Clarifying Questions
Clarification questions ask why something was said or how it relates. These questions help you develop a better understanding of the motive and meaning behind something.

Probe Assumptions
Probe Assumptions seek to fully define the assumptions being made. These questions ask for validation of assumptions, the consideration

Great coaches know how to ask the right questions. In fact, asking questions and listening to the responses is likely the most important aspect of coaching.

of alternative assumptions, or why certain methods were used (or not used). Asking such questions accomplishes two key goals. First, it helps you understand what has already been considered, and thus helps avoid repetition. Secondly, it pushes the one being asked the question to really think things through. If they have already thought about the things you are asking, they will already have answers to your questions, and it's entirely possible (if not likely) that your questions will drive them to determine next steps on their own.

Probe Reasons & Evidence

These types of questions will probe into reasons and evidences for claims being made. This would include asking for examples, root causes, or examples of why things are as claimed. A poorly conceived idea, or one that hasn't been explored yet, will have weak reasons and evidences. You might be surprised at how many problems are figments of imagination rather than actual problems. A well-conceived and thoroughly explored idea will have strong reasons and evidences.

Question Viewpoints & Perspectives

This line of questioning digs into viewpoints and perspectives. The intent here is to broaden the perspective, and to identify and consider the alternatives. By asking such questions, you draw out the biases that exist beneath the surface. We all have biases that cause us to naturally lean in one direction or another. When biases stay in the dark, they blind us and make it impossible for us to move past our own limited perspectives. When they are illuminated, alternatives can be justly considered and the direction we take will be strengthened.

Probe Implications & Consequences

In this type of questioning, we are striving to fully understand the implications and consequences of choices, assumptions, and alternatives. You may ask what the person is implying, or what the consequences of his or her assumptions may be, or what the implications of relating the current conversation with prior discoveries might be.

Questions about the Question

Asking questions about the question ensures that the focus of your discussion is actually on the correct topic. Does it matter? Does it add value? Does it apply? You may also ask the individuals you are coaching to ponder the reasons you asked a question in the first place. This will help them think more critically and ensure that they understand the question being asked.

Socratic Questions
Gain Clarification
Probe Assumptions
Probe Reasons & Evidences
Probe Viewpoints & Perspectives
Probe Implications and Consequences
Questions about the Question

How does all this effort in coaching our team members actually help us? It improves team and individual performance, it drives the team to make better decisions, and it develops a team of leaders that are individually and collectively capable of strong critical thinking.

Great coaching leads your team to think through issues and opportunities. This results in more effective planning, as well as more thorough execution. Performance will continue to increase and improve when plans are well laid out and execution is effectively managed

Good decisions require good information and good instincts. A team that is well coached will have the best possible information because they will think critically about every issue and opportunity. As experience with this process evolves, the team's instincts will also improve. Better decisions will result.

In the long run, this is the biggest advantage. A team full of leaders is a team that will win. This doesn't mean the team is all chiefs and no workers. Rather it means that every worker is both a team player and an independent thinker. It means that team members will rely on one another and will instinctively know when to ask for help or when to offer help. It means you won't have to make all of the decisions because the team will know the vision and be empowered to make the necessary decisions to bring the vision to reality. In other words, the effectiveness of leadership within the team will be multiplied rather than divided.

Being a great leader requires acting with intention. As John C. Maxwell said, "Action is what converts human dreams into significance."[92] Becoming a great leader requires acting on what you know needs to be done in an intentional way. Make a point to exercise the coaching skills needed to develop your team members. Be a coach and a mentor that causes those around you to increase in value—this will make you a highly valued leader.

Coach

Gives credit for success
Takes credit for failures
Listen Intently
Questions Everything
Provides Encouragement
Celebrates Wins
Provides Positive, Productive, Supportive
Reproof
Mentors

Passion

Many people believe that a leader is supposed to motivate the troops. I disagree. If your troops have to be motivated, you've got the wrong troops. However, the leader does need to provide inspiration. When the leader provides a purpose, or cause, that people can really latch onto—and an inspiring vision for what the future looks like when we live out that purpose—the team will be passionate about being involved.

Vision is all about strategic intent. "It is a dream that has been fashioned and molded into an image that can be communicated to others."[93] Because strategic intent is the desired or intended future result that is essential to the survival of the organization, it is where you and your team must be sharply focused.

The Vision Vector™

To further explore strategic intent, let's consider how "The Vision Vector" relates. In the mechanics of physics, there are scalar quantities and vector quantities. A scalar quantity is one that provides only magnitude. Speed or distance are examples of scalar quantities (e.g. travelling at a speed 70 mph, moving a distance of 10 yards). While these qualities provide detailed information about magnitude, they provide no information about direction. Vector quantities, however, define both magnitude and direction. Velocity and trajectory are examples of vector quantities (e.g. travelling at 70 mph at 315° from North, or 10 yards to the west). In other words, speed tells me how fast I'm moving, and heading tells me which direction I am travelling. Together, speed and direction make up velocity—a vector quantity.

Vision Vector™

When you have both a mission (direction) and objectives (magnitude), you have a vision.

Vision is a picture of the future (strategic intent) and to fully define vision, you need a strategic target [magnitude] and a strategic assignment [direction].

$$\vec{V} = (Objective, Mission)$$

Vision, or strategic intent, is a picture of the future. Therefore, to fully define vision, you need a strategic target [magnitude] and a strategic assignment [direction].

Blanchard Management Corporation teaches that "vision provides guidance for daily decisions so that people are aiming at the right target."[94] Bill Hybels notes that "Wise leaders understand that the single greatest determinant of whether followers will ever own a vision deeply is the extent to which those followers believe the *leader* will own it."[95] Therefore, a vision that provides direction and guidance is critical. As the developer of this vision, you MUST own it! You must embrace it, show passion for it, be zealous about achieving it, excited by the transformation that will result from it, and wholeheartedly strive to make it happen. Then, and only then, will those around you buy into that vision.

Strategic Assignment

A strategic assignment is the direction you will head as you work on living out your core purpose and fulfilling your vision. In other words, your strategic assignment is your mission.

To successfully complete a mission, you must have a team that accepts the mission and is passionate about completing it. If your team doesn't believe in the mission, you have three choices: [1] adjust the mission to be more inspiring, [2] convince the team of the mission's worth, or [3] replace the team (or portions of it).

Once you have a compelling mission and a team that is dedicated to fulfilling it, you're on the path to success. Your strategic plan will need to include at least one mission. Larger companies may be able to head in multiple directions simultaneously by placing different teams on different missions (while all are supporting the same purpose and vision). However, most teams and organizations will need to focus on a single mission.

A 'mission statement' is a great way for leaders to communicate this mission. It should

Mission

Strategic Assignment

It is the direction you will head as you work on living out your core purpose and fulfilling your vision.

The Direction of Vision

be short and sweet. A three-page mission statement is confusing, distracting, and will likely be counterproductive. Thus, a single sentence that summarizes the mission in a clear and concise manner is the best way to get the message across and keep it in the front of everyone's mind.

Strategic Target

A strategic target is the 'end-game' result that is essential to success. It is the objective or objectives that define successful completion of the vision. In this sense, it is the magnitude of the vision. A mission and its objectives go hand-in-hand. Defining either without the other provides incomplete information that doesn't paint the entire picture. When you have both a mission and objectives, you have a vision.

Objectives

Strategic Targets

Defines successful completion of the vision.

The Magnitude of Vision

As strategic targets, your objectives must be measurable and definitive.

As strategic targets, your objectives must be measurable and definitive. If they are vague and unclear, how will your team know when they have been accomplished? For this reason, every objective that you develop must define exactly how you and your team will know that the objective has been reached.

When developing your strategic plan, it is important to develop a number of objectives. Define your vision in stages of growth, such as a one-year plan, a three-year plan, a five-year plan, and maybe even a ten-year plan. You should have two or three objectives—that is two or three strategic targets—for each of these phases in your strategic plan.

To clarify, let's explore the difference between a goal and an objective. An objective is a strategic target. A goal, on the other hand, is a tactical target. Strategic targets are long-term and are essential to successfully accomplishing the vison. A tactical target, however, is important to a particular project or program, but is not necessarily essential to long-term success in reaching the vision.

Short and brief, your vision statement is a clear and succinct description of the Vision Vector™. It paints of picture of the future that depicts a completed mission and its associated objectives.

Passion
Inspiring Vision Vector™
Mission: Strategic Direction
Objective: Strategic Target

Persistence
Persistence requires an admission that challenges, hardships, and even suffering can lead to growth and development. In fact, it might be said that we can't learn without going through some difficulties or, at least, that the lessons learned from hardship are much more deeply ingrained within us. In this way, the obstacles we face in life are beneficial, if not essential, to our long-term growth and development. Consider these words of wisdom penned some 2000 years ago: "…we rejoice in our sufferings, knowing that suffering produces endurance; endurance produces character; and character produces hope."[96]

In his book, *David and Goliath: Underdogs, Misfits, and the Art of Battling Giants*, Malcolm Gladwell addresses this idea that hardships can actually produce advantages through lessons learned. He includes a three-chapter section called "The Theory of Desirable Difficulty" in which he relays three unique stories of individuals who accomplished great things due to adversity. He states that "what is learned out of necessity is inevitably more powerful than the learning that comes easily."[97] He recognized that those who learn and adapt when faced with challenges have a unique ability, and that this ability needs to be combined with persistence to yield memorable results. He said, "An innovator who has brilliant ideas but lacks the discipline and persistence to carry them out is merely a dreamer."[98]

So the obstacles we face in life, both as individuals and as organizations, are essential to building us up and making it possible for us to succeed. In a utopian world, we may be able to obtain success without challenge, but, on this side of heaven, no such world exists. So rejoice in your sufferings, face the challenges, build your character in the process, and create hope where none would otherwise exist.

The idea of persistence is simple. Getting things done requires a certain 'stickiness' from us that keeps us charging forward when others have long sense quit. It requires determination, stamina, fortitude, finesse, and perseverance.

Determination is rooted deeply in purpose. It is being completely certain of your purpose and mission and knowing how that mission will add value. It is a dogged unwillingness to give up fueled by a passionate belief in the cause.

As a leader, you must have that dogged unwillingness to give up—no matter what! If you don't, the challenges you will face will eventually overwhelm you, and you will quit. But if you do, those challenges will fail to hold you back.

During World War II, the Nazi empire pushed across Europe in an effort to overwhelm and destroy governments to take over the continent. Many showed great determination to fight against this fascism, and Winston Churchill is, perhaps, one of the greatest examples of its opponents. It was Churchill's sheer determination and will that made the United Kingdom fight back despite the barrage of bombings and the impending threat of invasion. His "never give in" attitude forged alliances, including the United States, that helped turn the tide and push the Nazi's back, ultimately defeating them.

Churchill had stamina, or staying power. It is an endurance that sees you through the most difficult of situations. Determination combined with stamina creates staying power; however, determination alone is never enough. Let me explain.

In athletics, stamina is developed over the long term. You don't just wake up one morning and have stamina. However, you may wake up with determination, which is essential to developing stamina. Building up your endurance requires diving head first into the pool of hardships, when you know full well that it's going to get miserable before it gets better.

As an example, I enjoy watching many of the obstacle course challenge shows that have been gaining in popularity. These shows challenge athletes—either individually, or as a team—to complete insane obstacle courses. Some of the obstacles are so challenging that I wouldn't expect anyone to be able to complete them, yet somehow, they do. The athletes overcoming these obstacles didn't develop the necessary stamina overnight. They trained hard for extended periods of time. They ate right, they worked hard, and they conditioned their bodies to possess the strength and endurance necessary to take on the course.

The same is true for you as a leader. Know that despite your objective, there will be challenges. You will need to dive into these challenges and find a way to get through them (or around them). Sometimes the best path involves climbing over the obstacles, sometimes you need to dig under, other times you need to tunnel through, and in some cases, you simply need to evade and go around them. The leader must decide which paths will be the most efficient route to achieving the objective and then rally the team to follow.

Going for it will require fortitude, which is the mental and emotional strength to carry on. Having fortitude doesn't mean you'll never have a 'breakdown', as breakdowns are just ways of releasing your pent-up emotions before carrying on with the effort.

While watching a recent episode of an obstacle course challenge, I saw a contestant fall (after getting a lot farther than 99.999% of the population would have gotten). I saw the emotional drain on her face and tears of disappointment. Moments later, while being interviewed, she was asked what this means to her career as a competitor. Until that moment she had been emotionally spent, the disappointment apparent in her posture. But when the question was asked, her posture changed and her countenance reflected a bit of confusion rather than disappointment. "I'm down, but I'm not out," she answered. "I just learned where I need to focus my training so I get farther next time." Now, that's fortitude. She's human enough to let her disappointment show, yet mentally tough enough not to allow the disappointment of failure to keep her from trying.

In addition to the determination, stamina, and fortitude necessary to keep going in the face of adversity, using finesse to handle challenging situations is extremely beneficial. Acting like a "bull in a china shop" may get you a lot of attention, but it isn't always the best approach. There are certainly times when such a shake-up is beneficial; however, most of the time, a more tactful and intelligent approach is advantageous, which can be labeled as finesse.

Finesse is about utilizing brain more than brawn. Finesse is akin to pacing yourself for a marathon, rather than sprinting to collapse before reaching the finish line. In the Bible, Goliath had brawn whereas David had finesse.

Finesse, then, can be defined as "intelligent tenacity"—or being tenacious with intention—a characteristic which produces winning results.

The characteristics of determination, fortitude, stamina, and finesse all feed a person's perseverance—or, his or her steadfast effort to plow forward despite seemingly insurmountable obstacles. Researchers from the University of Pennsylvania, the University of

Michigan, and the United States Military Academy, West Point have all studied what leads some people, and not others, to success. They questioned highly successful people in a number of fields. "Asked what quality distinguishes star performers in their respective fields, these individuals cited grit, or a close synonym, as often as talent. In fact, many were awed by the achievements of peers who did not at first seem as gifted as others but whose sustained commitment to their ambitions was exceptional."[99]

These researchers defined grit "as perseverance and passion for long-term goals," and noted that "grit entails working strenuously toward challenges, maintaining effort and interest over years despite failure, adversity, and plateaus in progress." They note that "the gritty individual approaches achievement as a marathon; his or her advantage is stamina…. the gritty individual stays the course."[100]

If, and when, challenges become overwhelming, taking a moment to examine and vent emotions may be necessary before getting back into the game. Viewing failures as lessons learned and learning from them contributes to better leadership. When leaders become intimately familiar with their purpose, and passionately dedicated to their vision, they have the fuel to cultivate the determination, stamina, fortitude, finesse, and perseverance needed to carry on and get the job done.

Persistence

Determination
Stamina
Fortitude
Finesse
Perseverance

Stick with it!
Success is waiting just around the corner.

Strategic Leadership

Strategic leadership is the foundation of STAR Leadership™. It is the combination of strong roots found in a firmly defined purpose and unshakable principles, and forward thinking demonstrated through passion inspiring vision and persistent effort. It is leadership that ensures your persistent effort is keenly focused within that vision that drives your passion. It is the leadership that places this vision within the non-negotiable principles that define and maintain your character. And, it is the leadership that ensures all of this is properly placed within your core purpose.

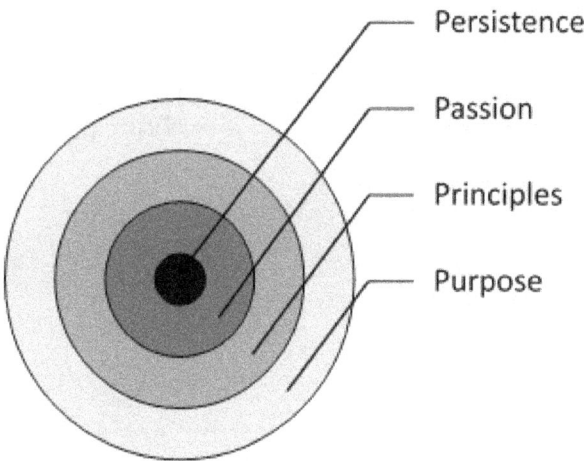

Persistence

Passion

Principles

Purpose

Figure 6. Concentric Circles of Strategic Leadership

As the "target" graphic demonstrates, our circle of persistent action must be centered properly, such that it becomes the 'bulls-eye' of the target. In fact, each level of these concentric circles must be placed fully within the circumference of the previous circle. **That is strategic leadership**.

When you allow your persistent action to get off center, such that part of your action is no longer focused on your passion inspiring vision, you effectively lose focus on making this vision a reality.

Even worse, when any portion of your action-circle resides outside the bounds of your principles-circle, you chip away at your character and lose far more than you gain. You may convince yourself that "the end justifies the means," but does it? Is your character worth what you get out of the effort?

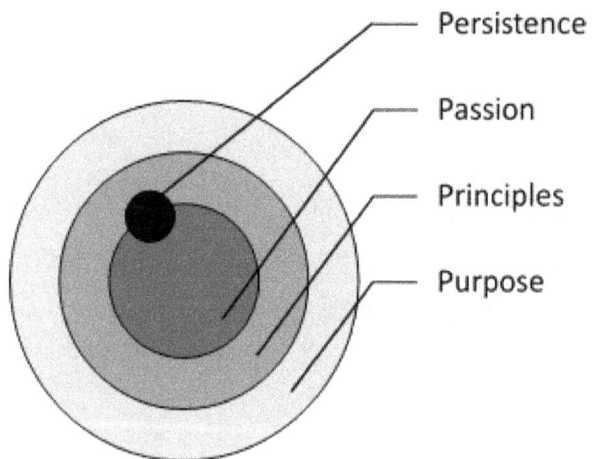

Figure 7. Off-Centered Circles of Unfocused Leadership

Similarly, when any of these circles move beyond the boundary of purpose we lose sight of why we are doing what we do. STAR Leadership™ can only occur when focus is maintained on the long-term objective. Keeping focus on the long-term objective requires a properly centered strategy…it requires strategic leadership.

This strategic focus is the Core Leadership Ideology of STAR Leadership™, and the concept behind its Core Leadership Theory (CLT), as defined by seven simple postulates:

1. A foundation of a worthy cause (purpose), rock-solid values (principles), and an inspiring vision (passion).

2. A calling to serve.

3. A strong focus on both results and relationships.

4. Intentional behavior & continual development.

5. Proactive alignment between the 'everyday' and the strategic ideology.

6. Behavior that is adaptable.

7. Coaching that encourages, empowers, and enables.

Your ideology is simply an understanding of core purpose, the clarity of principles that describes your character, and a vision that inspires passion in your soul and in the soul of your team.

It has been my intent that as you study through the content of this book you will develop a strong, focused, passionate foundation as a leader. You will need to spend some reflective time considering your personal purpose, and that of the organization that you serve (whether you are the founder or an employee, you have the potential to be a leader). Visit 2Xalt.com for helpful tools designed to guide you through this process, or contact 2Xalt, Inc. to schedule personal, one-to-one leadership coaching.

In the upcoming book, *Tactical Leadership*, I'll present follow-up ideas that extend the concepts of STAR Leadership™ from the foundation of the strategic, to the application of the tactical. I'll show you where your leadership should be focused, present some basic leadership processes that will improve the effectiveness of your leadership, and teach you some simple, everyday practices that will enhance your leadership efficiency and add value to you by helping you add value to those around you.

STAR Leadership™

PURPOSE

PRINCIPLES

PASSION

PERSISTENCE

LEADERSHIP

Strategic Leadership

Notes

[1] Northouse, Peter Guy. Leadership: Theory and Practice. Thousand Oaks. Sage, 2004. p. 3.

[2] Maxwell, John C. *Developing the Leader Within You.* Nashville. Thomas Nelson, 1993. p. 1.

[3] Carlyle, Thomas. "The Hero as Divinity." *Heroes, Hero-Worship, and the Heroic in History.* London. James Fraser, 1841. Web.

[4] Cherry, Kendra. *The Great Man Theory of Leadership.* 19 May 2016. About.com. 23 Feb 2016.

[5] Kotter, John P. *Leading Change.* Boston. HBR Press, 2012. p. 184.

[6] McGregor, Douglas. "The Human Side of Enterprise." *Adventures in Thought and Action: The Proceedings of the School of Industrial Management.* 9 April 1957. Cambridge: MIT. pp. 22-28.

[7] McGregor, Douglas. *The Human Side of Enterprise.* NY. McGraw-Hill, 1960.

[8] Ibid. pp. 33-34.

[9] Ibid. p. 35.

[10] Ibid. p. 47.

[11] "Genesis 2:15." *The Holy Bible.* English Standard Version. Crossway Bibles. 2001.

[12] McGregor. p. 47.

[13] McGregor. p. 47.

[14] McGregor. pp. 47-48.

[15] McGregor. p. 48.

[16] McGregor. p. 48.

[17] McGregor. p. 48.

[18] Cain, Susan. "Must Great Leaders Be Gregarious." *The New York Times.* 15 Sept 2012. Web. 24 Feb 2016.

[19] Rampton, John. "23 of the Most Amazingly Successful Introverts in History." *Inc.* 20 July 2015. Web. 24 Feb 2016.

[20] Fujioka, Russ. "How Bill Gates, Larry Page, and Mark Zuckerberg All Thrive as Introverts." *Inc.* 23 Feb 2016. Web. 24 Feb 2016.

[21] Grant, A. M., F. Gino and D. Hofmann. "Reversing the Extraverted Leadership Advantage: The Role of Collective Employee Proactivity." *Academy of Management Journal.* June 2011.pp. 528-550.

[22] "Analyzing Effective Leaders: Why Extraverts Are Not Always the Most Successful Bosses." 23 Nov 2010. *Knowledge@Wharton.* Wharton School, U. Penn. Web. 29 Feb 2016.

[23] Cherry, Kendra. "What is the Trait Theory of Leadership." *About.com.* 9 Jan 2016. Web. 23 Feb 2016.

[24] *PSYCH 485 Blog.* 5 Oct 2013. Penn State University. Web. 23 Feb 2016.

[25] Likert, Rensis. *Developing Patterns in Management.* NY. American Management Association, 1955.

[26] *ORG Module Unit 6: 6.4.2 Leadership Style*. University of Leicester. Web. 23 Feb 2016.

[27] Hersey, Paul and Ken Blanchard. *Management and Organizational Behavior*. Englewood Cliffs. Prentice Hall, 1988.

[28] *ORG Module Unit 6: Leadership, 6.4.1 Trait Theories*. University of Leicester. Web. 23 Feb 2016.

[29] Blanchard, Ken et al. *Leading at a Higher Level*. NY. Prentice Hall, 2007. Soundview Executive Book Summary, 2007.

[30] Blanchard, Ken, Patricia Zigarmi and Drea Zigarmi. *Leadership and the One Minute Manager: Increasing Effectiveness Through Situational Leadership*. NY. William Morrow and Co., 1985. p. 31

[31] Ibid. p. 35.

[32] Ibid. p. 39.

[33] Ibid. p. 32.

[34] Ibid. p. 35.

[35] Greenleaf, Robert K. "The Servant as Leader." *Servant Leadership: A Journey into the Nature of Legitimate Power and Greatness*. Ed. Larry C. Spears. NY. Paulist, 1977.

[36] see Luke 22:25-27

[37] Tzu, Lao. *Tao Te Ching*. Trans. John C. H. Wu. Boston. Shambhala, 2006. p. 35.

[38] *Star Trek II: The Wrath of Khan*. Dir. Nicholas Meyer. Perf. Leonard Nemoy. 1982. Film. <https://www.youtube.com/watch?v=Xa6c3OTr6yA>

[39] Lieberman, Matthew. "Should Leaders Focus on Results, or on People?" 27 Dec 2013. *Harvard Business Review*. 16 Mar 2016.

[40] Ibid.

[41] Blanchard, Ken, Scott Blanchard and Drea Zigarmi. "Servant Leadership." Blanchard, Ken. *Leading at a Higher Level*. Upper Saddle River. Prentice Hall, 2007. pp. 249-276.

[42] "Colin Powell." *Wikipedia*. Web. 29 Mar 2016.

[43] Powell, Colin and Tony Koltz. *It Worked for Me In Life and Leadership*. NY. HarperCollins, 2012. pp. 24-25.

[44] Ibid. p. 25.

[45] Ibid. p. 76.

[46] Thompson, Justin. *STAR Performance*. Nashville. WestBow, 2015.

[47] Powell and Koltz. p. 22.

[48] Giuliani, Rudolph W. *Leadership*. NY. Miramax, 2002. p. 115.

[49] "List of AFC Champions." *Wikipedia*. Web. 13 June 2016.

[50] "History, Pittsburg Steelers." *Steelers.com*. Pittsburg Steelers. Web. 13 June 2016.

[51] "Former Steelers Share Thoughts on Chuck Noll." *Steelers.com*. 14 Jun 2014.

[52] Maslow, Abraham H. "A Theory of Human Motivation." *Psychological Review* 50 (1943). pp. 370-396.

[53] Thompson. pp. 11-32.

[54] Ibid. pp. 49-52.

[55] Ibid. p. 10.

[56] *Constitution of the United States*. Congress of the United States, 17 Sept 1787.

57 Ibid. "Article V."
58 "Bill of Rights." The Amendments to the Constitution of the United States as Ratified by the States. NY. Congress of the United States, 4 Mar 1789.
59 *Captain America: The First Avenger*. Dir. Joe Johnston. Perf. Chris Evans. 2011. Film.
60 Scaglione, Robert and William Cummins. *Karate of Okinawa: Building a Warrior Spirit with Gan, Soku, Tanden, Riki*. NY. Person-to-Person, 1989. p. 33.
61 Powell and Koltz. p. 22.
62 "Proverbs 16:18." *The Holy Bible*. English Standard Version. Crossway Bibles. 2001.
63 "MLB Home Run Leaders (All Time)." *StatisticBrain.com*. Statistic Brain Research Institute. Web. 21 Sep. 2015.
64 "Babe Ruth Career Statistics." *StatisticBrain.com*. Statistic Brain Research Institute. Web. 21 Sep. 2015.
65 Powell and Koltz. p. 19
66 Maxwell, John C. *The 21 Indispensable Qualities of a Leader*. Nashville. Thomas Nelson, 1999. p. 77
67 "Proverbs 17:28." *The Holy Bible*. English Standard Version. Crossway Bibles. 2001.
68 Carnegie, Dale. *How to Win Friends and Influence People*. Pocket Books, 1981. p. 88
69 "6 Types of Socratic Questions." *Critical and Creative Thinking*. U. of Michigan, Web. 5 Oct 2015.
70 Carnegie. p. 220.
71 Ibid. p. 54.
72 Kotter, John. "The Key to Changing Organizational Culture." *Forbes Magazine* 27 Sep 2011. Web. 26 Oct. 2015
73 Funakoshi, Gichin and Genwa Nakasone. The Twenty Guiding Principles of Karate: The Spiritual Legacy of the Master. Kodansha, 2012. p. 97.
74 Watkins, Michael. "What is Organizational Culture? And Why Should We Care?" *Harvard Business Review*. 15 May 2013. Web. 26 Oct. 2015.
75 Thompson. pp. 11-32.
76 Kotter, John P. *Leading Change*. Boston. HBR Press, 2012. p. 184.
77 Collins, Jim. *Good To Great*. Harper, 2001. p. 74
78 SpencerStuart. "2004 CEO Study: A Statistical Snapshot of Leading CEOs." 200. Web.
79 Sanders, Jeffrey S. "The Path to Becoming a Fortune 500 CEO." *Forbes Magazine* 5 Dec. 2011. Web. 16 Nov 2015.
80 Powell and Koltz. pp. 20-21.
81 Ibid. p. 21.
82 Carnegie. p. 154.
83 Dale Carnegie & Associates, Inc. The Leader in You: How to Win Friends, Influence People, and Succeed in a Changing World. Pocket Books, 1993. p. 80.
84 Maxwell, John. *The 21 Indispensable Qualities of a Leader*. Nashville. Thomas Nelson, 1999. p. 74.
85 "Matthew 14:27." *The Holy Bible*. English Standard Version. Crossway Bibles. 2001.

[86] "Matthew 14:29b." *The Holy Bible*. English Standard Version. Crossway Bibles. 2001.

[87] "Matthew 14:31a." *The Holy Bible*. English Standard Version. Crossway Bibles. 2001.

[88] "Matthew 14:31b." *The Holy Bible*. English Standard Version. Crossway Bibles. 2001.

[89] Lindsey, Kevin. "John Wooden, Thank You for Being Such a Great Teacher." *Bleacher Report* June 2010. Web. 30 Nov 2015.

[90] "What is Socratic Questioning." *Socratic Questioning*. Science Education Resource Center, Carleton College. Web. 2 Dec. 2015.

[91] "6 Types of Socratic Questions." *Problem Solving*. Web. 2 Dec. 2015.

[92] Maxwell, John C. *Intentional Living*. Center Street, 2015. p. 15.

[93] Thompson. p. 13.

[94] Stoner, Jesse, Ken Blanchard and Drea Zigarmi. "The Power of Vision." Blanchard, Ken. *Leading at a Higher Level*. Upper Saddle River. Prentice Hall, 2007. 21-36. p. 26.

[95] Hybels, Bill. *Leadership Axioms*. Grand Rapids. Zondervan, 2008. p. 35

[96] "Romans 5:3b-4." *The Holy Bible*. English Standard Version. Crossway Bibles. 2001.

[97] Gladwell, Malcolm. David and Goliath: Underdogs, Misfits, and the Art of Battling Giants. NYC. Little Brown, 2013. p. 113.

[98] Ibid. p. 116.

[99] Duckworth, Angela L., et al. "Grit: Perseverance and Passion for Long Term Goals." Journal of Personality and Social Psychology 92.6 (2007): 1087-1101. Web. 14 June 2016. p. 1088.

[100] Ibid. p. 1087-1088.

Acknowledgements

I would like to thank my wife, Tanya, and kids, Joshua and Hannah, for their patience and encouragement as I've spent many hours preparing this text and the related course materials. Most importantly, I would like to thank the Father, Son, and Holy Spirit who have shown me the meaning of life. To some, this statement will make perfect sense, and to others, it will seem strange and foreign. The concepts of this text are powerful and applicable to your leadership ability regardless of your understanding or agreement with my relationship with God, however allow me to briefly explain how God has provided meaning.

In the beginning, God created mankind to resemble His own character, to represent His presence on earth, and to have a relationship with Him. This is our purpose. He tells us this in the first chapter of Genesis, which is the first book of His scriptures. He also tells us that our own sin – rejection of His instructions and directions for our lives – has destroyed our ability to live up to the purpose for which He created us. Because of sin – and we are all guilty of sin – none of us has the capacity to resemble His character, to represent Him, or even to have a relationship with Him – instead, we are condemned to an eternal death.

While this seemed hopeless up to this point, God provided hope in the form of His own Son who came to live as a man, die as a sacrifice for the sins of mankind, and rise from the dead to conquer death once and for all. To some, who misunderstand, this may seem elitist because belief in the Son, Jesus Christ, is the only way to restore our ability to resemble His character, represent Him on earth, and live in relationship with Him now and forever. Once we understand that we are condemned because of our sin, but that the Creator of everything sacrificed His Son to pay the penalty of our condemnation, so that we wouldn't have to, the sense of elitism fades in the face of God's love and grace.

To learn more and to request a free copy of Scripture, visit
2xalt.com/meaning-of-life.html

About the Author

Dr. Justin Thompson is a leadership expert, teacher, coach, and author. He has developed multiple courses and authored several books aimed at providing you with the tools you need to perform at a consistently high level, and to be a leader with high performance influence. Dr. Thompson is the founder and CEO of 2Xalt, Inc., an organization created to exalt the performance of individuals, teams, and organizations by providing leadership coaching and consulting services.

Dr. Thompson has over two decades of experience in various organizations including big business, small business, and start-ups. Through 2Xalt he has coached, trained, and consulted for multiple companies. He has help businesses optimize their organizational structure and operational processes. He has guided business through the launch of new products, and into new markets. He has help small businesses develop and communicate their business plan. He has offered multiple seminars to help organizational leaders and small business owners lead their teams effectively and perform at higher levels.

Visit 2Xalt.com to schedule Dr. Thompson for a seminar, webinar, leadership workshop, or consulting services.

Martial Art of Performance

Join the Leadership Development Program designed to develop Leadership 2Xalt Performance™. Our programs are designed to provide Education, Application, and Integration.

EDUCATION	APPLICATION	INTEGRATION
Builds knowledge by providing facts, information, and basic skills	Builds understanding through the development of comprehension, insight, and sound judgement	Leads to wisdom through cultivating a culture of discernment and action
Seminars, Books, Articles, and other Study Materials	Courses and Workshops	Leadership Coaching

Become Certified in STAR Leadership through mastering the concepts of Strategic Leadership, Tactical Leadership, and Performance Leadership.

Green Belt	Brown Belt	Black Belt
Master the concepts of Strategic Leadership	Master the concepts of Tactical Leadership	Master the concepts of Performance Leadership

Contact 2Xalt today and get started on your certification!

2Xalt.com

www.ingramcontent.com/pod-product-compliance
Lightning Source LLC
Chambersburg PA
CBHW032007190326
41520CB00007B/386